The SHERLOCK HOLMES file

'I enjoyed playing Holmes very much.'
HENRY OSCAR

'It was great fun to do.'
FELIX AYLMER

'Sherlock Holmes *was* larger than life.'
CLIVE BROOK

'I got no particular reactions out of it.'
RONALD HOWARD

'I want to make money on "Holmes" quick, so as to be through
with it!!'
WILLIAM GILLETTE

'You could never call him an attractive personality.'
CHRISTOPHER LEE

'I'm sure that on the face of it . . . Holmes *was* unpleasant.'
DOUGLAS WILMER

'I came to the conclusion . . . that there was nothing lovable
about Holmes.'
BASIL RATHBONE

'In my opinion he just seemed to be an insufferable prig.'
ALAN WHEATLEY

'When I did it, it was more melancholic, more disillusioned.'
ROBERT STEPHENS

'He obviously is a powerful projection of something in all of us.'
JOHN WOOD

The SHERLOCK HOLMES file

Michael Pointer

 Clarkson N. Potter, Inc./Publisher NEW YORK

DISTRIBUTED BY CROWN PUBLISHERS, INC.

By the same author

The Public Life of Sherlock Holmes
Hornsbys of Grantham

For Cicely

Library of Congress Cataloging in Publication Data

Pointer, Michael, comp.
    The Sherlock Holmes file.

    1. Doyle, Sir Arthur Conan, 1859-1930--Characters
--Sherlock Holmes. 2. Doyle, Sir Arthur Conan,
1859-1930–Illustrations. I. Title.
PR4624.P6 1976 823'.9'12 76-17464
ISBN 0-517-52560-7

First American edition published by Clarkson
N. Potter, Inc.

Printed in Great Britain

Contents

Introduction 6

The Formation of an Image 8

'Which of You is Holmes?' 26

Dogs in the Night-time 79

'My Friend and Colleague' 95

The Master of Disguise 106

Furnished Rooms to Let 115

In the Footsteps of Sherlock Holmes 135

Appendix 158

Acknowledgements 165

Index 166

Introduction

The scene is a familiar one, that we have seen, or read about, many times – a warm upstairs sitting-room on a foggy day in the eighteen-nineties. The typically over-furnished Victorian interior is completely untidy. The remains of a meal lie on the table, and tobacco smoke hangs in the air.

From outside there is the sound of horse hooves and the noise of iron-shod wheels scraping the kerb. A knock at the door, voices in the hall, footsteps on the stairs, and another client is ushered into the presence of the world's first consulting detective.

'I am Sherlock Holmes, and this is my friend and colleague Dr Watson . . .'

The game is afoot once more, and the story unfolds with the classic form and inexorable progress of a Greek drama, but the principal character has reached audiences in all walks of life, in every part of the world, and in dramatic productions that range to the farthest remove from Greek drama. Episodes in his imaginary life have been enacted so frequently that for some people it has become almost impossible to separate truth from fantasy any longer.

The many hundreds of genuine letters written to Sherlock Holmes in Baker Street demonstrate how surely the fiction has become fact. No other character in all the world's fiction has achieved such a penetration of the public's imagination, and to the entertainment industry the name carries virtual certainty of success.

This book is a pictorial survey of some of the ways in which Sherlock Holmes and his world have been presented and misrepresented to the public over the last ninety years or so, by artists, actors and dramatists. It is a world that has acquired an increasing fascination when viewed from our present trouble-torn times. Quite unintentionally Conan Doyle has given us a brief span of time preserved in amber, and it is because Sherlock Holmes is constantly examining details of everyday life that the whole period is evoked for us so vividly. 'Eight shillings for a bed and eightpence for a glass of sherry pointed to one of the most expensive hotels', explains Holmes in *The Noble Bachelor,* and we marvel at the picture it conjures up, as well as at the astute deduction.

Between 1974 and 1976 the amazing renewal of Sherlockian stage and screen activity has reminded us once again of the indestructibility of this remarkable person. As Orson Welles remarked, when introducing his own radio performance as Holmes in 1938: 'He is a gentleman who never lived, and who will never die.'

The Formation of an Image

The very idea of illustrated fiction presents a serious problem. The mind of an author meets the mind of a reader through the medium of the written word, and the resulting mental images vary according to the skill of the writer and the imagination of the reader.

The introduction of illustrations, particularly of fictional characters, can be very risky, and frequently proves a great disappointment. Sherlock Holmes is perhaps the most extreme example of how important the visual appearance of a character can become. In fact in Holmes's case his appearance is a hallmark now better known than the written words. Silhouettes of, say, Long John Silver, Mr Pickwick or Robinson Crusoe *might* be taken for other people. That of Sherlock Holmes is unmistakable.

The first illustrations of Sherlock Holmes accompanied the first story, *A Study in Scarlet,* in *Beeton's Christmas Annual* for 1887. They were by D. H. Friston and were not very successful. At that time neither was the story, and in spite of Conan Doyle's description (rather over six feet . . . excessively lean . . . sharp and piercing eyes . . . thin hawk-like nose) Holmes had acquired no special identity. The second story, *The Sign of the Four,* appeared in *Lippincott's Magazine* with similar results, and no depiction of the detective. It was not until July 1891, when the Sherlock Holmes short stories began appearing in *The Strand Magazine*, that a recognisable image began to emerge.

George Newnes had launched his magazine at a time of great advances in illustration printing and a corresponding expansion in periodical publishing, and although he was up against the competition of many similar publications (and some downright blatant copies), *The Strand* maintained its supremacy, and outlived practically all the opposition, for two main reasons: Newnes always had top authors and notabilities writing for the magazine, and *The Strand* was, in the words of its sub-title, 'An Illustrated Monthly.' There were very few two-page openings without at least one picture, and the quality of the layout and production was the best of its kind.

At first the editor agreed to take six of the *Adventures of Sherlock Holmes* by Dr Conan Doyle, who was finding authorship rewarding after the dismal failure of his medical practice. Illustrations were assigned to Sidney Paget; according to Paget's daughter Winifred, the editor intended to commission his brother Walter, but wrote in error to Sidney. It was a mistake that proved far-reaching in its

significance. As the late James Montgomery observed: 'What Phiz did for Pickwick, Paget did for Sherlock Holmes.'

The stories in *The Strand* were unexpectedly popular and gave a terrific boost to the sales of the new magazine in its first year. The set of six was hurriedly extended to a dozen, with Paget continuing as artist. He frequently used his unlucky brother Walter as a model for Holmes. By the time the twelfth story came out, the public, and the publishers, were clamouring for more, and Conan Doyle sensed that things were getting out of hand. Those Holmes stories were interfering with his other writings, which he regarded as much more important. He eventually agreed to a further twelve stories, now known as *The Memoirs,* but he was determined to put an end to Sherlock Holmes in the last one, ominously entitled *The Final Problem*, even if it meant burying his bank account as well.

In the fourth of the *Adventures* Sidney Paget had drawn a feature that, more than any other, was to become the trademark of Sherlock Holmes. The story was *The Boscombe Valley Mystery*, in which Dr Watson alludes to his friend's 'close-fitting cloth cap.' Paget drew it as a deerstalker hat such as he often wore himself, and at the time it passed unremarked. The pictures for that story were rather

above left: The first appearance of Sherlock Holmes, in every sense, in *Beeton's Christmas Annual.* Drawing by D. H. Friston

above right: George Hutchinson's frontispiece to the third edition of *A Study in Scarlet*

Dr Watson with Sherlock Holmes
in disguise, entering 221B Baker
Street (*A Scandal in Bohemia*); one
of only two Paget pictures showing
the exterior

above right: By the time of this
first appearance of the deerstalker
in *The Boscombe Valley Mystery*
the Holmesian profile was becoming
recognisably developed

Sidney Paget's very first picture just
happened to capture one of those
sublime moments by the fireside at
Baker Street

In this famous Sidney Paget illustration, as well as the others to *Silver Blaze*, Holmes again has his 'ear-flapped travelling cap' (but no Inverness cape, which may have originated with William Gillette), while Watson has the bowler which equally has become *his* inseparable symbol

murkily reproduced as half-tones, and not particularly striking. But nine stories later, when he drew Sherlock Holmes in a deerstalker again, for the story *Silver Blaze*, he produced one of the finest illustrations of the whole canon, and a depiction of Holmes and Watson that has seldom been surpassed. The picture is classical in content and execution: the two companions are seated in a railway compartment on one of their innumerable railway journeys; the composition is superb and the quality of the engraving is excellent.

Sidney Paget was not an exceptionally gifted illustrator, and at times his draughtsmanship leaves much to be desired, but his wistful, shadowy pictures evoke, as no others do, the twilight of the Victorian era, that charming gaslit, cobbled, horse-drawn world of Holmes and Watson 'where it is always 1895'.

In 1901 Doyle wrote *The Hound of the Baskervilles* (discussed later in this book) and it was serialized in *The Strand Magazine*. At the author's request the illustrations were again by Sidney Paget. With magnificent timing, the publication took place as William Gillette was taking London by storm with his melodrama *Sherlock Holmes*. The two successes complemented each other.

Earlier, when *The Final Problem* appeared, the story had graduated in position from somewhere in the middle to first item in the magazine, with a full-page frontispiece, a place Sidney Paget had not occupied before. When *The Hound* was published, the instalments occupied the prime position for 8 out of the 9 issues involved, with a frontispiece each time.

Throughout this period Arthur Conan Doyle was pouring forth

a succession of short stories, novels and articles, practically all of which made their first appearance in one or other of the profusion of monthly magazines. But all the time there came an incessant demand for more Sherlock Holmes. Even if Holmes *were* dead at the foot of Reichenbach, and many found it hard to accept, there were numerous unreported cases to which Watson had carelessly alluded in the existing stories. Why could they not be written, just as *The Hound* had been?

Doyle had to surrender. The next series *The Return of Sherlock Holmes* was inevitable. Of course, Paget continued as illustrator and during this period October 1903 to December 1904 he produced some of his best work on this subject, as well as his last, for he died in 1908. After Paget there was no regular illustrator, but then there was no regular output of the stories either. Conan Doyle took 22 years to produce the remaining 20 Holmes adventures. But with Sidney Paget's total of 356 illustrations to 38 stories the pattern had been set, and all his successors were obliged to observe it. Among his successors, that same Walter Paget who had missed the job of illustrator was given it for one story only, in December 1913, when he drew 4 pictures for *The Dying Detective*. One of the most striking of the post-Paget artists was Frank Wiles, who drew a remarkable, vividly-coloured frontispiece for *The Valley of Fear*, which began in *The Strand* in September 1914. This picture, sometimes wrongly attributed to Sidney Paget, is one of the most frequently reproduced of all the illustrations, and shows Sherlock Holmes in strong profile. The shape of the head is perhaps a little

H. M. Brock illustrated only one story in *The Strand*, but his best depiction of Holmes was on this cigarette card in the 1930s

Arthur Twidle's superb illustration to *The Red Headed League* only appeared in book form. He was the first artist to succeed Paget in *The Strand*, and one of the best, but he only illustrated two stories for the magazine

distorted, but the angle of the face and the forcefulness of the painting cause us to overlook that.

It fell to Frank Wiles to illustrate the final three stories when they appeared in 1927. He could not have known that *Shoscombe Old Place* would be the end of the saga when he re-introduced the deerstalker on Holmes in his pictures for that story. It had not been thus seen in *The Strand* since Paget drew it in 1904; it was a fitting way to close the long and remarkable association of the magazine and its most remarkable personage.

In the USA the first publication of the stories was a haphazard affair, with various appearances in newspapers and magazines. Consequently a tradition of the appearance of Holmes and Watson took much longer to form, with round-faced all-American youths contrasting with occasional importations of some of the Paget drawings. Not until Frederic Dorr Steele began supplying illustra-

For a number of years the less-frequently appearing Holmes stories were reserved for the sumptuous Christmas double numbers of *The Strand*. The adventure for December 1913 was *The Dying Detective*, the only story illustrated by Walter Paget

The famous Frank Wiles frontispiece to *The Valley of Fear* was the only coloured picture to adorn a Holmes story in *The Strand*. It was also reproduced on the magazine cover

Travelling again – Holmes and Watson in a cab with Inspector Macdonald by Frank Wiles (*The Valley of Fear*)

Holmes based on Gillette, by
Frederic Dorr Steele

tions for *Colliers Weekly* in 1903 was there a distinctive depiction
in print in America. Steele acknowledged that he based his conception on the appearance of William Gillette, frequently using
photographs of the actor as a guide. Steele's indebtedness to Gillette
is interesting because, although Paget was the originator of the
deerstalker for Sherlock Holmes, William Gillette was almost certainly the person most responsible for popularizing it, throughout
his triumphs on the stage, and so it was further popularized by
many of Frederic Dorr Steele's drawings.

While there is no denying the ability and craftsmanship of Steele's

The last appearance of the deerstalker in the last picture of the last story. *Shoscombe Old Place*, illustrated by Frank Wiles in The Strand, April 1927

work, a lot of which was done for later book issues, his illustrations have acquired a reputation that is rather disproportionate to their real worth. Apart from Steele there has been no really outstanding American illustrator of the tales, although, as in Britain, there have been occasional artists with considerable sympathy for the subject.

But beyond the problems of depicting Sherlock Holmes on paper lie the immense difficulties of portraying him in the flesh. This has now been done frequently enough for it to be clear that an actor faces the role with severe limitations placed on the interpretation he can give. He is expected to conform to the Holmesian conventions, and if the dramatist concerned has not observed these conventions closely the actor has an almost impossible task.

The first case. Sherlock the undergraduate in *The 'Gloria Scott'*

Impressing the client at the start – a favourite Holmes gambit. Here he shatters Mr Grant Munro's incognito in *The Yellow Face* by reading Munro's name on the lining of his hat

More deduction from a hat (*The Blue Carbuncle*)

It is, perhaps inevitably, back to Sidney Paget that so many trails lead, especially today when the Victorian aspect of the Holmes genre is now so well admired. The appearance of Holmes, and Watson, as drawn by Paget has established a standard by which not only other illustrations are measured, but also the presentations of actors undertaking the role. 'People had remarked so frequently: "You really ought to play Sherlock Holmes. I've never seen anyone so like Sidney Paget's drawings",' said Arthur Wontner. 'I tried to take the make-up and so on from the first illustrations by Sidney Paget,' said Alan Wheatley. 'I got it together from the Sidney Paget pictures and Conan Doyle's own descriptions,' said John Wood.

Conan Doyle's lack of enthusiasm for Sherlock Holmes never really left him, and consequently he seldom showed much keenness over the various portrayals of his celebrated character. In a rare moment of approbation, in a speech in 1921, he said: 'If my little creation of Sherlock Holmes has survived longer perhaps than it deserved, I consider that it is very largely due to those gentlemen who have, apart from myself, associated themselves with him,' and he went on to praise most generously the work of Sidney Paget as well as the impersonations of a number of actors.

In the section *Which of You is Holmes?*, portraits are included of 'those gentlemen who have associated themselves' with Sherlock Holmes, whether they resembled the image formed by Sidney Paget, or by Frederic Dorr Steele, or no particular conception.

Sherlock Holmes – pioneer forensic
detective (*The Naval Treaty*)

Brother Mycroft

'I can never resist a touch of the
dramatic' – returning the stolen
papers to Phelps in *The Naval
Treaty*

Holmes the lover of beauty:
admiring a rose in *The Naval
Treaty* . . .

. . . and dreamily enjoying a concert
in *The Red-Headed League*

Holmes on the receiving end for
once: from the Cunninghams in
The Reigate Squires

'Professor Moriarty stood before me' – Paget's depiction of the arch-villain

Awaiting the showdown by the Reichenbach Falls

'Which of you is Holmes?' – enter
Dr Roylott in *The Speckled Band*

Getting down to the job (*The
Boscombe Valley Mystery*)

The eagle eye at work in Regent Street . . .

The master disguised as 'a common loafer' in *The Beryl Coronet* – 'a perfect sample of the class', marvelled Watson

. . . and spotting the depressing effects of hotel pen and ink in *The Hound of the Baskervilles*

opposite: First appearance of the hound (April 1902). Compare this with pages 83, 86 and 91

Publishers Ward, Lock & Co used illustrations by James Greig for some later reprints of *A Study in Scarlet.* See the same scene on page 117

Classic profile: pondering the mystery of *The Man With The Twisted Lip*

'Which of You is Holmes?'

We all have our favourites among the interpreters of the Great Detective, and this gallery of impersonators contains illustrations of many of those actors who have tackled this most difficult role.

Pride of place naturally goes to the first actor to portray Sherlock Holmes in public, Charles Brookfield. With his fellow humorist, Seymour Hicks, he wrote an 'extravaganza' called *Under the Clock* which formed part of a triple bill at the Royal Court Theatre in 1893. The piece made great fun of Holmes's detection and Watson's devotion ('Oh Sherlock, you *won*derful man!' sings Watson at one point), and Brookfield and Hicks played these roles with great gusto. Apart from being very entertaining, *Under the Clock* showed how famous Sherlock Holmes had become by that time.

By far the most celebrated stage Sherlock Holmes was the American actor William Gillette, and his melodrama, *Sherlock Holmes,* is by far the best-known Holmes play. And it even turned out to be the biggest success of the Royal Shakespeare Company at the Aldwych Theatre in London in 1974, some seventy-five years after the play was first performed in New York.

William Gillette was already a famous actor-playwright, and achieved a great personal triumph in his melodrama *Secret Service,* before the even greater success of *Sherlock Holmes,* which he wrote with Conan Doyle's consent. Right from its triumphant opening in New York in 1899 the play was unstoppable. Gillette appeared in it in London in 1901 and 1905, and in tours and revivals in America. Translations and piracies of his play were presented in numerous parts of the world, with many of the actors in this portrait gallery in the title role.

The financial rewards from all this success enabled William Gillette to build himself a remarkable dwelling at Hadlyme, Connecticut, that has become a form of American stately home called Gillette Castle, regularly thronged with tourists. Gillette's career was considerably affected by his success in the role, because the close association of character with actor had become legendary, and it was a measure of his extraordinary popularity in the part that when he was coaxed out of retirement in 1929 to give a farewell tour in *Sherlock Holmes,* the unprecedented occurred. So enthusiastic was the reception that Gillette was obliged to continue the tour through three seasons, until 1932.

Finally, in 1935, he performed in the play once more, on radio for CBS. He had already been the world's first radio Sherlock

Holmes in 1930, when his prestige gave a great send-off to the first radio series of Sherlock Holmes adventures. On and off he thus appeared in his own play for a period of 36 years, undoubtedly the longest span of portraying Sherlock Holmes that there has been.

P. M. Stone described a performance during that last stage tour as one of the most thrilling and memorable events he ever experienced in the theatre:

'On Gillette's first entrance, as he slowly removed his overcoat and seated himself at the foot of the staircase . . . the entire house stood up and, after an impressive moment of silence, extended to the distinguished actor a tumultuous greeting in tribute to the genuine affection and admiration in which he was held.'

27

Essanay
GEORGE K. SPOOR PRESIDENT

The wonderful work of Britain's most remarkable Detective in Fiction has been visualised in a Film of supreme merit.

Sherlock Holmes

is a Seven-act Master Drama, in which William Gillette plays the role he created on the stage.

The Greatest Screen Story yet offered

Throughout his career as Sherlock Holmes on the stage Julian Royce had the misfortune to play second fiddle, or smoke second pipe as it were, to H. A. Saintsbury. They both began as Holmes in March 1902 in separate Charles Frohman companies that toured the Gillette play in Great Britain; Saintsbury in the North Company and Royce in the South. Saintsbury went on to make the character of Sherlock Holmes very much his own, appearing in a film and on the West End stage, as well as touring for nearly two decades, while Royce is now mainly forgotten.

The first and second Frohman tours lasted until May 1904, after which Julian Royce left, and a Midlands Company was formed, led by Kenneth Rivington as Holmes. Saintsbury and Rivington continued touring in the play until June 1905, by which time Saintsbury had given 936 performances in the title role.

In 1910 when Conan Doyle hurriedly wrote and presented a stage

Gillette and supporting cast at the
Lyceum, September 1901, as
caricatured in *The Stage*

"SHERLOCK HOLMES" AT THE LYCEUM.

version of *The Speckled Band*, H. A. Saintsbury was chosen to play
Sherlock Holmes in the original production at the Adelphi Theatre,
London. It was soon apparent that *The Speckled Band* was set for a
successful run in the West End, and the first touring company was
hastily organised, commencing at Blackpool with Julian Royce back
again playing Holmes. Royce toured in *The Speckled Band* until
early 1911, when he appears to have given up the role for good.

Like William Gillette, Saintsbury made only one venture into
motion pictures and, like Gillette, it was in the role of Sherlock
Holmes. In Saintsbury's case it was the first film version of *The
Valley of Fear*, made in 1916, and like many stage actors he did not
take easily to the medium of the silent picture, although the film
was successful. Ironically, one person who could have given Saintsbury some help with movie acting was Charles Chaplin, who by
that time was the world's highest paid entertainer, and who had

Julian Royce   H. A. Saintsbury

been given his first chance on the legitimate stage by Saintsbury in 1903 when he was cast as the page-boy Billy for the second tour of the North Company.

In an interview in 1916 Saintsbury revealed how closely he was identified with his most famous part: 'Yes, I have often been taken for Sherlock Holmes. Little boys, especially when I have been travelling in the provinces, call out the name after me. Once I even had the police call on me to help them solve a case. So I have always taken a special interest in acting Sherlock Holmes, and no doubt it was partly owing to my resemblance to Conan Doyle's creation that I was first asked to play the part'.

The stage production of *The Speckled Band* was revived in London in 1921, at the time of the Stoll series of silent Holmes pictures, and in 1929 Saintsbury again toured in *Sherlock Holmes*, at the time of Gillette's own farewell tour in the USA.

When the original Charles Frohman tours of Gillette's play ended in 1905, Harry Yorke, proprietor of the Theatre Royal, Blackburn, acquired the rights and resumed the touring of the play using some of the members of the old Frohman companies, including H. Lawrence Leyton as Sherlock Holmes. Leyton had begun touring in the play with the North Company as Forman the butler in 1902. Later he became Dr Watson to Saintsbury's Holmes, and finally

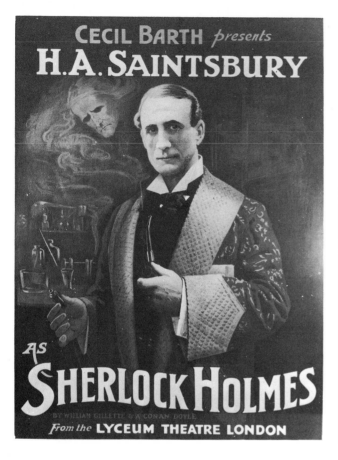

graduated to the title role in Harry Yorke's company, having with
him Master Charles Chaplin as Billy. Chaplin had returned to the
provinces, after tasting success in the West End with Gillette at the
Duke of York's Theatre in 1905, and both he and Leyton finally
left Yorke's tour early in 1906. Later, when *The Speckled Band*
transferred from the Adelphi to the Globe Theatre in 1910,
Lawrence Leyton re-appeared as Dr Watson, thus finally accom-
plishing a West End part soon after Saintsbury himself.

left: A mystic poster for
Saintsbury's performance

H. Lawrence Leyton

When it comes to the question of who has given the *most*
performances as Sherlock Holmes, one tends to think of William
Gillette as the record-holder, with H. A. Saintsbury as a respectable
runner-up. But after the Frohman and Yorke tours ended there
came on the scene a lesser-known actor named H. Hamilton Stewart,
who had earlier played the part of James Larrabee in an Australian
tour of Gillette's play in 1902. Stewart began touring the same play
with his own company in September 1906 and continued until 1917
or 1918. Apart from the sheer stamina and mental endurance
involved in such an accomplishment, Stewart must have offered a
considerable portrayal as Sherlock Holmes to have secured bookings
and return bookings for so many years. In a 1907 report *The Stage*
said: 'Mr H. Hamilton Stewart gives a fine and well-defined sketch
of the astute detective. Holmes's perfect *sang-froid* and indifference

H. Hamilton Stewart

to danger are naturally portrayed and, while playing with perfect ease, Mr Stewart at times rivets the attention of the audience, especially in the scene in which Professor Moriarty visits Holmes in his rooms'.

Understandably, Hamilton Stewart must have flagged a little in his dedication to the role. In 1913 he began alternating the Gillette play with *Alias Jimmy Valentine*, which he gave for the first half of the week, keeping *Sherlock Holmes* for the second half with the Saturday night audience. Stewart may well have found relief in playing a character on the wrong side of the law, for Jimmy Valentine was a gentleman-crook somewhat in the style of Raffles, and his adversary, incidentally, was a detective named Doyle!

Stewart seems to have continued doubling these plays throughout most, if not all, of the Great War period, and probably sometime in 1918 he finally ended his tours as Holmes. Since it is not clear how many times he presented both plays in a week, it is difficult to know the exact total of Stewart's appearances but it seems likely

Firmin Gémier

that he played the role something like 2,000 times, compared with about 1,300 by Gillette and approximately 1,400 by Saintsbury.

Ferdinand Bonn was the proprietor of the Berliner Theater in Berlin where, in 1906, he presented his own play *Sherlock Holmes*, in which he played the title role. 'It proved a splendid advertisement for the piece,' said *The Era*, 'that the Crown Prince not only attended the performance twice, but on the second occasion filled the stalls with the soldiers of his company, treating them in the entr'acte to beer and sandwiches in the theatre garden.'

Equally successful was Ferdinand Bonn's sequel *Der Hund von Baskerville*, which is discussed in the section *Dogs in the Night-Time*. Bonn later re-appeared as Sherlock Holmes in silent films, in a single film for Vitascope, *Sherlock Holmes contra Dr Mors*, about 1914, and finally in 1918 in a short series of films made by the Kowo company.

A fascinating translation of Gillette's play was the French version by Pierre Decourcelle in which the famous actor Firmin Gémier

33

Viggo Larsen with revolvers in
*Sherlock Holmes contra Professor
Moryarty* (Vitascope, 1911)

soared into one of the greatest successes of his career. Gémier had a fine flair for melodrama and the play suited him perfectly. The dramatic intensity with which he invested the role of Sherlock Holmes was described in contemporary reports as quite astonishing. Although perhaps not much like the Sidney Paget depiction of Sherlock Holmes, Gémier was certainly an acceptable Holmes in France, and appeared in the loud check cloth cap that Continental countries associated with *le détective amateur*.

The production became the talk of Paris and according to Gémier's biographer, Paul Blanchart, it was for decades afterwards a legend in the French theatre. It opened in December 1907, ran for 335 performances, was revived in April 1909 and again in 1912. In each of these productions Gémier was extremely fortunate in having an actor of the calibre of the great Harry Baur as his Moriarty – a major factor in any successful version of the Gillette play. By one of those strange and illogical pieces of casting that have bedevilled Sherlock Holmes dramatisations from the beginning, it was Harry Baur who appeared as Holmes in the final revival of Decourcelle's play in October 1915; but doubtless the pleasure-seeking poilus thronging the theatres in the Great War were not unduly critical of that.

The first Sherlock Holmes impersonator to appear in a *series* of films was Viggo Larsen, who acted in six films which he directed for the Danish company Nordisk in 1908 and 1909. When he left

Holmes is Stapleton's prisoner in the first *Der Hund von Baskerville* (Vitascope, 1914); Alwin Neuss doing the suffering

Denmark he became a leading actor-director in German films, eventually running a film company in partnership with the dramatic actress Wanda Treumann, but his first work in Germany was with Vitascope, for whom he directed in 1910 a highly successful series of five films called *Arsène Lupin contra Sherlock Holmes,* in which he again played Holmes. The following year he appeared in a single Holmes film, *Sherlock Holmes contra Professor Moryarty* (*sic*), also for Vitascope, and in 1918 he appears to have given his final portrayal of Holmes on the silent screen in *Rotterdam – Amsterdam.* Although none of Larsen's Holmes films has survived, the few stills that exist show him as a smartly-dressed master of the situation, and it seems likely that he too based his portrayal on William Gillette.

Alwin Neuss was another of the early actor-directors who very quickly mastered the technique of the silent picture, and proceeded to turn out scores of good quality films. None of them became classics, to be listed in film histories, but they provided a regular flow of good entertainment. (It is worth remembering that some very old films may have become classics simply because they are the only examples of a given type or period to have survived.)

During his distinguished career in films, Neuss had a fairly extensive run as Sherlock Holmes, whom he first played for Nordisk in Denmark in 1910, after Nordisk's first Holmes, Viggo Larsen, had gone to Germany. Neuss soon went to Germany himself, where he played in *Der Hund von Baskerville* for Vitascope. He followed this with four sequels to *Der Hund* before he left to go to another company, where the first film he made was another Sherlock Holmes adventure, *Ein Schrei in der Nacht* (A Scream in the Night). This was expensively produced for its time and featured, as was customary in the earliest movies, a Holmes who was more a frantic man of action than anything else. With a big eye on the American market, the story was set in a New York which had both Bond Street and Wall Street, and the climax was a grand chase and shoot-out at a hunting lodge in Bishop Creek in the Yosemite valley.

Sad to relate, Alwin Neuss, who became a prominent director and star for the Decla company, forsook Holmes and played an imitation-Holmes detective in a series of 'Tom Shark' films!

After 1911 authors had better copyright protection so far as films were concerned, and in 1912 Conan Doyle sold Sherlock Holmes film rights to the French company Eclair for what he regarded at

Georges Treville

the time as a handsome payment. The company made eight two-reel films at Bexhill-on-Sea with what they claimed was an all-English cast. They kept very quiet about the fact that the principal character in the series, Sherlock Holmes himself, was played by a French actor, Georges Treville, who also directed the series. Shooting of the eight films, each about twenty minutes finished length, took place over a thirteen-week period from May to August 1912, and Treville filmed most of his exteriors in the locality. Part of the Bexhill Kursaal was converted to a studio for all the interiors.

Despite the flamboyant advertising claims that the films were made under the personal supervision of Conan Doyle, there is no evidence that he went anywhere near Bexhill, which is rather surprising since they were the first Sherlock Holmes films made in Britain. Doyle makes no reference in his memoirs to the identity or

James Bragington

appearance of the actor playing Holmes, and one cannot help wondering what he thought of the rather swarthy-looking slightly-built Treville. It could have been part of the deal with Eclair that Treville both acted and directed. The only aspect of these films that Doyle *does* mention is the financial one.

The next person to play Sherlock Holmes in a British film was not an actor at all, although he was English. James Bragington happened to be an accountant working for G. B. Samuelson, who was about to make the first film version of *A Study in Scarlet* in 1914. George Pearson, the director, recounted how the casting came about:

I particularly wanted someone who fitted the image of Sherlock Holmes – tall and thin, narrow-faced and so on, and I couldn't

A wonderful detective story that's distinctly different

SIR A. CONAN DOYLE

A Study in Scarlet

By Sir A. Conan Doyle

Writer of the World's Most Fascinating Detective Stories

Gold Seal-Universal. 2 reels. Released Dec. 29th, 1914—featuring that popular Universal Star, Francis Ford. This is first of a series of fascinating, mysterious detective stories by the noted author, Sir Arthur Conan Doyle, in which Sir Arthur shows himself at his best. It is a story of the supreme cleverness of Sherlock Holmes in which is unraveled a tale of human suffering and in which an innocent man nearly suffers for the crime of the guilty one. The masterful style in which this absorbing plot is told in pictures will hold your audience spellbound. It is a picture with a punch, action, dramatic intensity, romance and cleverness. Sir Arthur Conan Doyle's fame as a writer of absorbing detective stories is world wide. It's a privilege to be able to book such a production. Book it NOW. 1-3-6 sheet posters. Advertise it in a big way. You're bound to play to capacity crowds with this big 2 reeler. Wire or write your Exchange immediately.

Universal Film Manufacturing Co.
Carl Laemmle, President
Largest Manufacturers of Films in the Universe

1600 Broadway   **New York**

Francis Ford

find anyone that looked the part. And then I remembered this man in Samuelson's Birmingham office. He wasn't an actor, but I was able to direct him all the time you see, because it was a silent film, and it worked very well.

It was Bragington's only acting role, and he was never heard of again.

Meanwhile in America the world-famous film director John Ford had begun his movie career in 1913 as a labourer and then as a third assistant prop man with his older (by thirteen years) brother Francis Ford, who was an actor-director under contract to Universal. In those pioneer days of silent serials and series films Francis Ford and Grace Cunard were extremely successful practitioners of exciting crime and adventure films. A frequent arrangement was for

Eille Norwood in the play *The Return of Sherlock Holmes*, 1923

Grace Cunard to write the scenario, Ford to direct, and both of them to play leading roles. In December 1914 Universal presented a two-reel version of *A Study in Scarlet*. True to form, Grace Cunard had written it, and Francis Ford directed and played Sherlock Holmes. Whether Conan Doyle knew anything of this film is doubtful, even though his photograph was used in the advertising. Certainly it must have been a very abbreviated adaptation of the story. (Although he never reached stardom, Francis Ford worked in movies all his life, and right up to his death in 1953 played character parts in the classic Westerns made by his younger brother John.)

The most frequently filmed Sherlock Holmes of all was Eille Norwood, who acted the part in 47 silent movies. This astonishing total comprised three series of short films, each of 15 stories, and

FACE TO FACE

EILLE NORWOOD

S.H.

H G STOKER.

MY DEAR WATSON

ERIC STANLEY.

LAUDERDALE MAITLAND. HILDA MOORE. STAFFORD HILLIARD. ARTHUR CULLIN.

"THE RETURN OF SHERLOCK HOLMES" AT THE PRINCES.

Sending up *The Return*, the caricaturist pays tribute to Eille Norwood's magnetism in the role (*The Stage*)

two feature-length films, all made between 1921 and 1923. Despite the quantity and rate of production, the quality was extremely good and the films were deservedly successful.

Conan Doyle wrote his *Memories and Adventures* at that time and gave warm praise in that volume to Norwood's portrayal of Sherlock Holmes. As Doyle's *Memories* were first serialized in *The Strand Magazine* while the films were showing, the publicity probably benefited the film-makers. Norwood really deserved Conan Doyle's commendation; coming to the screen from a lengthy stage career he quickly mastered the technique of silent film acting, and carefully underplayed his part as the master detective, distinguishing himself from the members of the supporting casts, many of whom overacted like mad.

'The last thing in the world that Holmes looks like is a detective' said Norwood. 'There is nothing of the hawk-eyed sleuth about him. His powers of observation are but the servants of his powers of deduction, which enable him, as it were, to see round corners, and cause him incidentally to be constantly amused at the blindness of his faithful Watson, who is never able to understand his methods.'

Immediately the films were completed and issued Eille Norwood appeared in *The Return of Sherlock Holmes*, a stage play specially written for him, and after the triumph of the films the play had a ready-made success and coasted through the West End and on tour with the greatest of ease. The same play was performed in Amsterdam in 1924, with Henri de Vries as Sherlock Holmes.

Henri de Vries using his pipe as a gun in *The Return of Sherlock Holmes*, Amsterdam 1924

In America, Sam Goldwyn produced a silent film of the Gillette play. His director, Albert Parker, described how it came about:

> I was in the revivals of the William Gillette plays, in small parts, and *Sherlock Holmes* was one of them. That was when Gillette was touring in the States. I loved the Sherlock Holmes stories as a boy, really loved them . . . When I became a film director, I had made a number of films and I went to see John Barrymore in his theatre dressing-room when he was appearing on the stage. I forget the play. I told him that I wanted to make a film of the Gillette play and I wanted him to play Sherlock Holmes . . .
>
> He didn't want to do the film. I had to talk him into it. He didn't like the part, because it was such a trade mark . . . In the

The Great Profile: John Barrymore
versus the bizarre Moriarty of
Gustav von Seyffertitz in the film
Sherlock Holmes (Goldwyn 1922)

end he said he'd do it. So immediately I took a train all the way
to Chicago to see about getting the rights to the play, because
when I saw Barrymore I didn't even have the rights! Anyway I
did get the rights; you know, maybe I still own *Sherlock Holmes*
and somebody else is making all the money from it!

Considering all the trials he underwent with his star, Albert
Parker managed to accomplish a very good and successful picture,
which he looked back on with great fondness.

Back in England, Edward Stirling had had a small part in the
1921 revival of *The Speckled Band* at the St James's Theatre, and
acquired a liking for the play that never left him. His one-time
colleague Henry Oscar recalled the subsequent events:

It came about in 1922 when Edward Stirling and I were acting
together at Hanwell, and we decided to form a company of our
own. To finance it each of the eight actors concerned put up £50,
which was a considerable sum for an actor to find in those days.
We called ourselves The London Players, and were not very
successful at first, so we decided to go on tour. This went very
well and eventually we had four different companies on the road
in entirely different styles; one performing Shakespeare, one giving

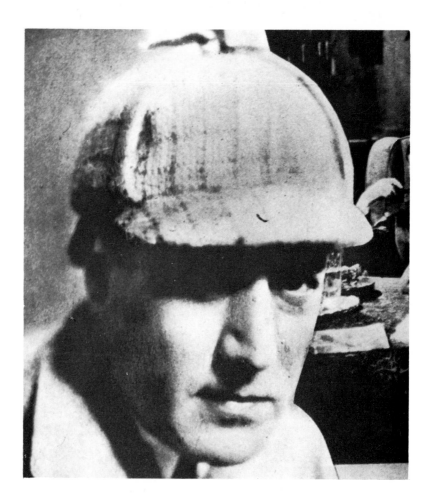

Carlyle Blackwell

The Speckled Band, one doing comedies, and I forget the fourth. Edward Stirling was more concerned with the business side of things, while I concentrated on direction.

We toured in *The Speckled Band* for most of 1922. Stirling played Roylott and I was Holmes. His wife (Margaret Vaughan) and my wife (Elizabeth Dundas) alternated in the role of Enid Stonor. You see, we both had young families at the time and so they took it in turn to tour for a few weeks at a time, bringing the children with them . . . *The Speckled Band* was a good play for Stirling and me. It provided a good balance of contrasting parts, and I enjoyed playing Holmes very much. Stirling modelled his performance on Harding's to an extent. You know, Harding was a fine actor in the grand style; full of good dramatic actions and poses. We went to France after touring England, and amongst other things we did *The Speckled Band* in Paris, in English. Stirling stayed on and in fact remained in Paris for the rest of his life. After that I moved on to other things . . .

From about 1911 the American film actor Carlyle Blackwell was seldom out of work. His name turns up in film after film among the

early silents, frequently as the dashing romantic hero. By the middle 1920s he was making films in Europe. Then came the talkies and, as with many silent stars, his career was virtually over, but at least he had the distinction of being the last Sherlock Holmes in silent movies, in the 1929 *Der Hund von Baskerville*.

H. Reeves Smith (Watson) and Clive Brook consider the body-in-the-library cliché in *The Return of Sherlock Holmes* (Paramount 1929)

The next large step – the first Sherlock Holmes talking picture – was made by Paramount in the same year, with the already celebrated Clive Brook as the Master. As might have been expected, he carried off the part with his customary polish and dry wit, and he repeated his stylish performance three years later in a second Holmes film for Fox. He confirmed the deliberate emphasis and humour of his portrayal:

I may be all wrong in that, but that's how I looked at it, because Conan Doyle wrote a figure bigger than life, there's no question about that. It was exaggerated, and I took advantage of that, especially in the first film, and it certainly came off, that first one, from the reception of the audience. They loved it, because there were a lot of laughs in it . . .

Sherlock Holmes *was* larger than life – I've seen so many good

actors play the part straight, just exactly straight, as a very clever detective; perhaps they've played the violin a bit or something, but to me they've never got the full dimension of his character.

I remember going to the preview of *The Return of Sherlock Holmes* with members of the studio and to our amazement there was laugh after laugh after laugh – a little bit because I exaggerated it, and I was rather pleased with the film in a way, because it had gone down well. They enjoyed the humour of it, you see, without losing the drama. I wasn't able to do it in the second film so much. That was a terrible film . . . Reginald Owen is a very good actor, but the part he had as Watson was nothing, really.

In fact, Reginald Owen is unique in having played both Dr Watson *and* Sherlock Holmes on the screen. As Watson to Clive Brook's Holmes in 1932 he really did have an insignificant part that was obviously only included as a mere formality. In *A Study in Scarlet* the following year, Reginald Owen was cast as Holmes in a lively adventure film that owed nothing to Conan Doyle and had little of Sherlock Holmes in it either. In spite of that it was a well-made movie, and Reginald Owen's performance was fairly good, considering that his appearance, voice and acting style were all against him in the role.

In his stories Conan Doyle actually retired Sherlock Holmes from his Baker Street practice, and had him keeping bees at a little dwelling on the Sussex downs. Occasionally his tranquil privacy was

interrupted by some vital and pressing matter that others could not manage, and such was the case in the 1933 stage play *The Holmeses of Baker Street*. Felix Aylmer was an aged widower Holmes who was determined not to become involved with crime again and resolutely refused to let his brilliant daughter, named Shirley (what else?) take up detection either. Despite a much-praised performance by Felix Aylmer, and a warm reception generally for the play, this comedy-drama never had the success that its skill and humour merited.

Once sound films had got under way, companies busied themselves with re-making silent successes as talkies, and out of the abundance of Sherlock Holmes movies of the 1930s there emerged a cluster of gems in the form of five films featuring Arthur Wontner as one of the greatest of the impersonators.

It is hard to write about Arthur Wontner's portrayals of Holmes without an excess of superlatives. After a string of Holmeses of assorted shapes and styles, and mostly disappointing, his appearance in *The Sleeping Cardinal* in 1931 tended to make enthusiasts light-headed in their response. Fortunately the film itself was good as well and its success led to sequels, all of which showed Wontner's Holmes as a developing and fascinatingly acceptable person; a gentler, mellower Holmes than many we have seen, but a character of great intellectual strength.

Many of us were in such a daze of happiness at witnessing the sort of portrayal we had long despaired of seeing that perhaps we

opposite, top: Reginald Owen in *A Study in Scarlet* (World Wide 1933)

opposite, below: Arthur Wontner, Ian Fleming (Watson) and Minnie Rayner (Mrs Hudson) in *The Sleeping Cardinal* (Twickenham Films 1931)

THRILLS!
ACTION!
SUSPENSE!
MYSTERY!

GILBERT CHURCH & J. C. JONES present
ARTHUR WONTNER *as Sherlock Holmes and*
IAN FLEMING *as Dr. Watson*
in the film version of SIR ARTHUR CONAN DOYLE'S *most popular story*

THE TRIUMPH of SHERLOCK HOLMES

Publicity for Wontner in *The Triumph of Sherlock Holmes*, based on *The Valley of Fear*

would not have noticed if the film *had* been poor. As a matter of fact it was awarded the New York Cinema Critics prize for the best mystery film of the season. 'It was the first British talkie to go over big, as they say, on Broadway,' said Mr Wontner. 'I had a screen test with about a dozen other actors down at Twickenham, and I was chosen by Julius Hagen to play Holmes . . . I knew the stories very well. You couldn't say I was an expert or anything like that, but I liked them very much, and it helped with getting the dialogue right. I found quite a lot of dialogue in the stories that we were able to use. Of course Leslie Hiscott had done a good job of the script, with another writer, but I was keen to see that the dialogue was authentic. Yes, I did enjoy working with Hiscott; I think he was the best director I worked under.'

Leslie Hiscott directed two more of the Wontner Sherlock Holmes films, and all five of the series were well-made and successful at a time when British film making was at a low ebb.

Bruno Güttner in *Der Hund von Baskerville* (Ondra-Lamac-Film 1937)

I happened to be with Arthur Wontner during the opening of the 1951 Sherlock Holmes Exhibition at the Festival of Britain, when one of the exhibition organisers brought a reporter to meet him. 'This is Mr Arthur Wontner,' said the organiser, 'who has appeared in *five* Sherlock Holmes films.' I noticed the reporter laboriously misspelt his name in her notebook. 'Oh yes,' said the reporter to Wontner, 'and what part did *you* play?'

I have never been able to discover the reason for a strange group of three Holmes films all appearing in Nazi Germany in 1937. It seems an odd sort of coincidence if three different organisations decided independently to make a film with Sherlock Holmes, all at the same time. First by a short muzzle was yet another *Der Hund von Baskerville*. (See 'Dogs in the Night-time', page 79.)

In the second film Herman Speelmans appeared as Jimmy Ward, a chubby-faced debonair young man moving in high society, and the infiltrator of a criminal gang. He turned out to be Sherlock Holmes,

Herman Speelmans (Neue Film 1937)

Hans Albers (Ufa 1937)

working in league with the secret police. It seemed a clear case of merely using the great name to sell the picture, which was called *Sherlock Holmes: Die Graue Dame* (The Grey Lady). The film would have been no different without the great name. And Holmes working with the secret police? Well, really!

Der Mann, der Sherlock Holmes war was a remarkable piece of light fantasy to have been produced in Germany at all, let alone in 1937. Hans Albers and Heinz Rühman, both popular stage and screen actors, had an enjoyable time impersonating Holmes and Watson when they were really a couple of confidence men at large. They eventually wound up in court and a character calling himself Sir Conan Doyle (*sic*) testified that they do not exist.

Although the various productions of *The Hound of the Baskervilles* are dealt with elsewhere in this book, the 1939 film of the story is very important because of the first appearance of Basil Rathbone as Sherlock Holmes. It was superb casting, made at a time when Rathbone was rising in star status. The sweeping success of *The Hound* brought in its wake an immediate sequel, *The Adventures of Sherlock Holmes,* and these two Twentieth Century–Fox films were stylishly made, beautifully mounted in Victorian

period costume and thoroughly satisfying as Sherlock Holmes movies. They also had splendid performances by Rathbone. His brisk self-assurance and elegant style were wholly in keeping with the late-Victorian characterization, and he presented Holmes as a convincing and thoroughly enjoyable personality.

The outcome of the two Fox films was a long-term contract for Rathbone to play Sherlock Holmes on the radio, followed by a long-term contract from Universal for 12 more Holmes films. They were commitments that Rathbone lived to regret:

> The continuous repetition of story after story after story left me virtually repeating myself each time in a character I had already conceived and developed. The stories varied but I was always the same character merely repeating myself in different situations. My first picture was, as it were, a negative from which I merely continued to produce endless positives of the photograph.

Rathbone's films for Universal were an unhappy series of adaptations, set in the 1940s and often in incongruous surroundings. Roy William Neill made a brave attempt at directing poor material, but

The classic team of Nigel Bruce and Basil Rathbone in *The Adventures of Sherlock Holmes* (Twentieth Century–Fox 1939), with Ida Lupino and Alan Marshall

Rathbone and Bruce as they appeared in several of their films for Universal. (*Punch* remarked on 'The locks of Sherlock')

right from the outset they were B pictures, and that was no good for Rathbone's career either. He grew extremely resentful of the situation:

> In due time, and not unreasonably I think, these endless repetitions forced me into a critical analysis of Holmes that was often disturbing and sometimes destructive. For instance, towards the end of my life with him I came to the conclusion (as one may in living too closely and too long in seclusion with any one rather unique and difficult personality) that there was nothing lovable about Holmes. He himself seemed capable of transcending the weakness of mere mortals such as myself . . . understanding us perhaps, accepting us and even pitying us, but only and purely objectively.

Seven years after the end of the film contract, which he had refused to renew, Basil Rathbone unwisely attempted a comeback as Sherlock Holmes in a stage play written by his wife. It was a lamentable failure, lasting only three nights on Broadway.

On television the first *series* of Sherlock Holmes adventures was a set of six programmes transmitted live by the BBC in 1951, with

Alan Wheatley as Holmes. He had no fond memories of the role at all:

Alan Wheatley in *The Reigate Squires* (BBC Television 1951), with John Vere (butler), H. G. Stoker (Colonel Hayter) and Raymond Francis (Watson)

'I was doing a lot of television at the time, and I did something, I think it was *Rope*, and C. A. Lejeune gave me a marvellous notice in *The Observer* and she finished up by saying "If the BBC have got any sense they will commission a series of Sherlock Holmes stories and ask Mr Wheatley to play Sherlock Holmes". So the BBC, very unlike them, took this up and wrote to her and said "All right, if you will do the scripts we will do the series," and that's how they came to be done . . .

I have to admit that I absolutely hated the plays. I never enjoyed doing anything less. I wish I didn't feel like that about it, but it remains a very unpleasing memory, because of the dialogue and construction. I never felt right in the part. I didn't want to play it in the first place, because I'm not a Holmes addict. I enjoy the stories, but I'm not an addict by any means . . . I don't think that they would ever have cast me if it hadn't been for Lejeune having put it like that, and then when they commissioned her to do it I'd more or less got to play it . . . In the books Holmes has a certain modicum of humour that just saves him, but in these

Alfred Burke (Photo: Lisel Haas)

scripts there wasn't a vestige. In my opinion he just seemed to be an insufferable prig . . . I think it also did me a lot of harm. It did have an enormous amount of publicity, which rather went to my agent's head and he started asking very much bigger salaries for me, and really dished my television career.'

Alfred Burke, the Frank Marker of television's *Public Eye,* acted in a rare revival of Gillette's play *Sherlock Holmes* given by the Birmingham Repertory Theatre for a month in 1952:

'It seemed to us at the time an unusual choice. It sounds a bit like Sir Barry Jackson, doesn't it? When we read it, it promised to be much more enjoyable than one would have thought. I mean, to do a dramatization by an American, no less, of a couple of the Holmes stories strung together with a funny love interest in it, which we skirted round. *We* cut out those bits of dialogue that referred to that . . . We did it straight as a detective melodrama, without any comic overtones. The love interest is an absolutely preposterous idea! It's so un-Holmesian. Even if you know very little about Holmes, it's untypical . . . We had a very good company up there at that time, you know. Paul Daneman was Dr Watson, Alan Bridges was Moriarty . . . It played very well as a piece, as long as one played it wholeheartedly, which we did. We

had a marvellous time doing it, and *I* had a marvellous time reading all the stories again to give myself a background, and provid-
ing myself with a Persian slipper for the tobacco and all that kind
of thing.'

In the USA, television in the 1950s was served by repeated show-
ings of the Rathbone films, and a long series of half-hour adventures
specially filmed for American television. The Sherlock Holmes in
the latter was English actor Ronald Howard:

'This American Sheldon Reynolds came over here looking for
someone to play Holmes, and I got the job. I went to France at
the beginning of 1954, and then the family came out and I was
there for a year. We moved abroad, sold our house and went to
Paris, lock, stock and barrel. They had to operate from Paris
because they hadn't got any studios in London.
 We did 39 episodes and came home. Then there was a lot of talk
of repeating it, but it didn't repeat. It would have been complicated because of moving and living abroad again. I don't think
we could have gone on doing them indefinitely; frankly, my
feeling was that it was of limited possibilities. We could only use
so many of the original stories. Reynolds bought some of them
from Adrian Conan Doyle, who lived in Switzerland. Adrian sold

56

him about three or four, I think, and Reynolds got some kind of rights in the title so that he could use a number of original scripts. He employed some American writers who were living in Europe to do these stories . . . Later he parcelled them up into a number of features from which he made a lot more money – for himself. We gained nothing because it was before residuals came in . . . I got no particular reactions out of it. I just played it the best I could. It was *intended* to be a younger Holmes and Watson. They'd always cast someone older for it before. Boney (Howard Marion Crawford) was a very good choice for Watson.

opposite: Christopher Lee and Thorley Walters (CCC Film 1962)

You must realise we were churning these films out at the rate of one every four days; it was really breakneck speed. That's one thing I particularly remember about it. It was a terribly concentrated effort to keep going at all. After about six months I was becoming dead beat. There was scarcely time to learn the lines. I used to get up early in the morning to learn them, before I went to the studio, because fortunately they didn't start work until midday. About 12.30 they would start, by which time all the crew would have had lunch, and then you worked through until 7.30 or 8.00 at night. It was pretty hectic, and also we were often motoring off to other locations. It was fun, but it was a very far from ideal way of going about it. It was far too rushed.'

It took a very long time for someone to think of casting as Sherlock Holmes the tall, gaunt English actor, Christopher Lee, and when it happened in 1962 it was, in his own words:

'. . . in a very indifferent picture . . . It was done in Germany with a German producer who had no idea at all about how to present anything of Victorian England on the screen, so he had all the wrong music, and all the wrong attitude towards it . . . Thorley and I were, I think, very well cast as Watson and Holmes. We were the only two English people in it (the rest were all Germans), wearing a German idea of how Holmes and Watson should dress, made by a German tailor, the whole thing went slightly too far and became very bizarre and slightly unreal, and the story was quite ludicrous. If you add this understandable lack of period knowledge on the part of the Germans (why should they know) to the attitude that doesn't care whether it is true to the original and faithful to the conception, you're bound to get an indifferent result, which is indeed what happened . . . I shot it in English; they dubbed it into German, and various other languages, but when they showed it in England it was not my voice. They got an actor to dub *me* in English, although I'd shot it in English! . . . To me, Holmes is a cold man; he is dedicated to the pursuit of criminals, he is a great patriot, he is totally intolerant, he doesn't suffer fools, he is not hypocritical, he is totally truthful, totally honest, totally direct, but you could never call him an attractive personality. Admirable, yes; you can respect him, you can admire him, you can fear him, but you cannot have a feeling of warmth towards him . . . I played him as a man of tolerance, irritation, tremendous speed of speech, such is the vast quantity of brilliant ideas flashing through his brain all at the same time; a man who was capable of the power of deduction that Conan Doyle wrote as the classic feature of Sherlock Holmes.'

For the record, the film was entitled *Sherlock Holmes und das Halsband des Todes*, and had an understandably brief life on release in England and the USA as *Sherlock Holmes and the Deadly Necklace*. It had an odd ending in which the necklace is recovered, but Moriarty goes scot-free. If the film company did this with a

Nigel Stock and Douglas Wilmer in the Sherlock Holmes pub, London, at the time of their 1965 BBC television series

sequel in view, they never mentioned it to Christopher Lee, and they never made one.

On BBC television Alan Wheatley was succeeded in 1965 by Douglas Wilmer, whose series of 12 adaptations was a little variable, but generally made with a sincere and sensible approach.

Said Douglas Wilmer: 'I had always very much wanted to do it, in fact, I applied to do it. It wasn't going to be a series originally, just one, *The Speckled Band*, but it was a prospective pilot . . . I think that any series must be something of a nightmare to anybody who's playing a pretty considerable part, particularly if it's anything carrying a great deal not only of weight and length responsibility but also of reputation responsibility. I don't mean my reputation, I mean the reputation of Holmes. You're not dealing with a character who's just been dreamt up by somebody yesterday, but with somebody who's known in various translations from Dan to Beersheba. One felt the burden of that.

Andre Morell (Watson) and Peter
Cushing in *The Hound of the
Baskervilles* (Hammer 1959)

I found it was a great strain . . . It is impossible not to if you're
playing Holmes and doing something which is cold-hearted, such
as the half seduction of a servant girl in order to get into Charles
Augustus Milverton's house, which shocked Watson very much.
Watson could say, in his narrative, "If I didn't know that under-
neath that cold and aloof exterior beat a heart that is as warm
and true as," whatever the line is. But you cannot do this in a
dramatisation. All you're left with is the cold and aloof thing and
the behaving in a dastardly fashion, because you're seeing Holmes
doing it without seeing it through Watson's eyes, and this is the
chief difficulty. In fact I think you could complain that my
Holmes was unpleasant. I'm sure that on the face of it, except to
the people who knew him extremely well, Holmes *was* unpleasant
. . . It didn't mean that he had no heart, and in the books, you
see, Watson says that he has. Watson softened the impact'.

(Wilmer had the misfortune to reappear as Holmes in a rather feeble comedy film, *The Adventure of Sherlock Holmes' Smarter Brother*, made by Gene Wilder in 1975. Luckily for Wilmer he was not required to be on the screen for very long in that adventure.)

When Douglas Wilmer's TV series was repeated in 1966, its great success was rather unexpected by the BBC, and they began to consider another series, which eventually appeared in 1968 with Peter Cushing as Sherlock Holmes. It was an unhappy presentation, trading on Cushing's reputation in sensational movies, as well as the popular fashions in violence and sex.

'The final test of fame,' wrote H. L. Mencken, 'is to have a crazy person imagine he is you.' It's been happening to Napoleon for years, so we are told, and it finally happened to Sherlock Holmes in 1961, in James Goldman's play *They Might Be Giants*, in which a New York judge, disturbed by the death of his wife, believes that he is Sherlock Holmes, engaged on a crusade against the forces of evil.

The play was presented at Joan Littlewood's famous Theatre Workshop at Stratford, East London, and the would-be Holmes was played by Harry H. Corbett, better known as Harold Steptoe. He recalled:

George C. Scott and Joanna Woodward in *They Might Be Giants* (Universal 1972)

60

'It wasn't intended to have a long run. It was part of the season, and whatever had happened we would not have gone to Broadway with it. Not only that, but it wasn't that big. We didn't have the money to do it as it should have been done. I don't think it was a success as a film either. It had a lot of whimsy in it; maybe that's why . . . It really dealt specifically with the American way of life . . . the play was full of references, marvellous for Americans, they recognised them immediately, but the theatre audiences here, they just didn't know what it was about. It was part of American theatre. American theatre has got a history of this kind of satire, and a lot of it goes straight over our heads . . . The play was beautifully written and constructed. His morality and his ideas were very good.'

Despite the play's lack of success it was later made into a charming, but equally unsuccessful film, with George C. Scott in the principal role. It was a performance of finely-judged control, and demonstrated a flair for comedy that Scott has seldom been allowed to display on the screen. A consummate stage actor, Scott held together the delicate structure of Goldman's flimsy tale with deceptive ease, and Anthony Harvey's skilful direction pointed up

John Neville and Donald Houston in *A Study in Terror* (Compton – Sir Nigel, 1965)

all the Holmesian conventions that were subtly woven into the plot.

In 1965 a company called Sir Nigel Films was formed by the Sir Arthur Conan Doyle Estate to be responsible for the filming of Conan Doyle's works. Their first venture, made for them by Compton-Cameo, was *A Study in Terror*, from an excellent original script by Donald and Derek Ford in which Sherlock Holmes solved the mystery of the Jack-the-Ripper atrocities.

This fine film was well publicised as a Holmes movie ('Spell it with excitement – the name is SHERLOCK HOLMES'), but hardly any prominence was given to the actor concerned, John Neville. Although he has appeared in several films, he is much better known for his stage performances, particularly in Shakespearean roles. On this occasion he gave an extremely good brisk portrayal of Sherlock Holmes, at times reminiscent of Basil Rathbone in the delivery of his lines. His grave demeanour and cool self-confidence was relieved by the humour of other characters in the film, rather than from any lightness given to Holmes himself. Neville subsequently played Holmes on the stage when he took over the leading role from John Wood in the RSC New York stage production.

'When *I* did it, it was more melancholic, more disillusioned,' said Robert Stephens (who in fact followed John Neville in the same stage production):

The accelerated smoking machine produces a selection of tobacco ash for Robert Stephens in *The Private Life of Sherlock Holmes* (Mirisch 1970)

'In the film the idea Billy Wilder wanted to explore was why did
Holmes have this disdain for women; why did he take drugs; why
did he live with Dr Watson; was he homosexual or not. That's
why the film was called *The Private Life of Sherlock Holmes,*
because in the book there is never revealed any of that. He said
to me "You must play it absolutely seriously. You must never
send up Dr Watson, never make fun of him . . . It must be a love
affair between two men," which indeed it is. It's like Raffles and
Bunny, this odd relationship that men have. Not that Sherlock
Holmes is a homosexual, but he has a distrust of women. The
press made a lot of that, but if the other sequences had been kept
in, that wouldn't have been so important, because we had a
wonderful sequence in flashback that explained *why* he didn't
trust women. Billy and Izzy made up that in his youth he had
been very much in love, as a student, with a young girl who
finally turned out to be a prostitute. That just finished him. And
it was just *cut*, which I thought was very sad because it was a
charming sequence.

Sherlock Holmes has always fascinated Billy, because Billy is
somebody who gets on frightfully well with men, and he was
fascinated by the relationship between the two men . . . I was
cast first and he said "You can't have Laurel without Hardy.
Now we have to find Dr Watson" . . . and he cast Colin Blakely,

John Wood and Nicholas Selby
(James Larrabee) at the Aldwych
Theatre, 1974

63

which I wanted him to do, because we have done many plays together and you have inbuilt a relationship and a respect and an affection between two people. You're halfway there. The relationship between Holmes and Watson has to come across as a believable relationship. It must do. One can't exist without the other. It's like two sides of a coin.

The marvellous thing about Billy is that he will see a sequence and say "We can do it better, and *I* can do it better. I will rewrite the dialogue. It could be better." But I mean you have to be Billy Wilder to be able to spend that amount of money and have a flop, which it was. It cost about nine million dollars, and it hasn't made its money back.

The final picture was a frightful mess, because half of it was cut. As it is, the film doesn't make any sense . . . It was a great disappointment to me, because to play Sherlock Holmes day in, day out, for 29 weeks on a movie set, you are so sick of Sherlock Holmes by the end of it that you never want to hear the name

Once more into the breach in cape, cap and lens: Richard Franklin in *Sherlock Holmes of Baker Street,* Ipswich Theatre-Go-Round, 1974

mentioned again, but you hope and think it will be entertaining and successful, and it may be worth it.'

The revival of William Gillette's play in London in 1974 was the signal for a staggering renewal of interest in Sherlock Holmes on the stage. The Aldwych production of *Sherlock Holmes* was taken to New York, where John Wood and the RSC players packed the theatre for months.

Riding on the tail of the Aldwych triumph came a cheeky piece called *Sherlock's Last Case* (see the section *My Friend and Colleague*), with Julian Glover as a supremely conceited Holmes. Then, at the end of 1974, the Nottingham Playhouse presented a revival of Conan Doyle's *The Speckled Band* with Donald Gee as Sherlock Holmes. This production dithered between straight melodrama and send-up, and so failed to convince either way.

In 1975 John Southworth adapted three of Doyle's short stories under the title *Sherlock Holmes of Baker Street* and presented them at the Ipswich theatre with much-deserved success. The Sherlock Holmes, well studied and played with a nice sense of humour in his relationship with Watson, was Richard Franklin.

Apart from the actors in the text and captions of this section, there are some who appear in other sections, and there are those in the check list of portrayals about whom we know so little that they are now just names in the record. But altogether they constitute the most complete record of Holmes' impersonators.

'Which of you is Holmes?' demanded Dr Roylott when he stormed into the Baker Street rooms in the story *The Speckled Band*. Well, which of these actors has *been* Holmes? It is, of course, largely a matter of personal preference, as with all dramatisations of fictional favourites. Whether you have looked for a frantic man of action, succeeding largely by brute strength and coincidence, or for a steely-eyed scientific reasoner, only resorting to physical activity to demonstrate the infallibility of his deductions, or for a character somewhere between these extremes, the presentations of Sherlock Holmes have included most categories. Very few of them have been strictly in accordance with what Conan Doyle intended but then Sherlock Holmes himself has developed into something much more than Doyle envisaged. He is one of those rare characters in fiction who take on separate existences beyond the control of their creators and become literary immortals, capable of activities and adventures quite outside the works of their original creators.

But in spite of that, Conan Doyle's basic conception of Sherlock Holmes, and the accepted conventions which early on became closely associated with Holmes, have to be observed if a satisfactory dramatisation is to be achieved.

As the drama critic of *The Liverpool Mercury*, said in 1901, writing about the first appearance of Gillette's play in Britain: 'The placing upon the stage of figures beloved in the pages of fiction more often than not results in the destruction of preconceived ideals and the despoiling of memories.'

A Belgian actor of note, Marcel
Myin appeared as a guest star in
the first production in Holland of
Gillette's *Sherlock Holmes* in 1902

This trio provides a souvenir of an
evening in Stockholm (24 April
1902) when all three performers
coincided in their appearances in
the Gillette play at three different
theatres! Left to right, actors
Bergendorff, Bergrall and Nyblom

Another of the many touring Holmeses was Herbert Bradford in *The Speckled Band* (1912)

Charles Conway, quick-change
artiste and impersonator, as
Holmes in 1902

First Holmes on the Danish stage
was Dorph-Petersen in the Gillette
play (1901)

Otto Lagoni, seen here in the
Gillette play at the Aalborg
Teater, Denmark, in 1902, was
probably the first actor to play
Holmes on both stage and screen

Another Danish stage Holmes: Vilhelm Birch at the Aarhus Teater (1902)

The name of the first film Holmes, shown in this frame enlargement from *Sherlock Holmes Baffled* (1900), remains a mystery

Harry Benham, a regularly-featured leading player with the Thanhouser film company, appeared just once as Holmes in *Sherlock Holmes Solves the Sign of the Four* (1913)

Hugo Flink as Holmes in the first
series of Sherlock Holmes films
made by Kowo-Film AG in
Germany (1917)

In Conan Doyle's one-act play *The Crown Diamond,* performed in the early 1920s as part of a variety programme, the part of Holmes in this unfortunate piece was played by Dennis Neilson-Terry

Lyn Harding, the original Adelphi Theatre Dr Roylott of 1910, was pitted against the Holmes and Watson of Raymond Massey and Athole Stewart in the only sound version of *The Speckled Band* (B & D 1931)

Geoffrey Edwards in the revised version of *The Return of Sherlock Holmes* at the New Theatre, Bromley (1953)

opposite: Radovan Lukavsky (Holmes) and Vaclav Voska (Watson) in the Czech film *Touha Sherlocka Holmese* ('Sherlock Holmes's Desire'), 1971

Diana Lambert (Helen Stonor), Alan Moore (Holmes), and Michael Keating (Watson) in *The Speckled Band* at Manchester Library Theatre, 1970

Tim Preece in *The Hound of the Baskevilles,* Perth Repertory Theatre

Peter Bayliss (Watson), Barbara New (Mrs Hudson) and Julian Glover in *Sherlock's Last Case* at the Open Space Theatre (1974)

Dogs in the Night-time

In Victorian fiction, particularly in the works of such authors as Charles Dickens, widespread use was made of what is nowadays known as the flashback. At some point or other in the story the narrative would stop dead, and a seemingly fresh tale would begin, often recounted by one of the characters, and often supplying the background and motivation for the story that has been mystifying us thus far.

At its worst the flashback is a clumsy disruption of the narrative flow that sometimes occupies a disproportionate amount of the complete book, and can be very tiresome for the reader. In its most highly developed form, in films and television, the flashback is a deft, dramatic device that can enlarge and illuminate the plot to a tremendously exciting degree.

Two of the four Sherlock Holmes long stories, *A Study in Scarlet* and *The Valley of Fear*, are encumbered with lengthy flashback sections, while a third, *The Sign of Four*, has a somewhat shorter one near the end. Only *The Hound of the Baskervilles* has a continuous narrative, and only *The Hound*, out of the four long stories, has been such a popular subject for dramatisation. Right from its inspired title to its thrilling climax the story remains on a far higher level of excitement than almost any other tale in the Holmes saga, and throughout the piece Conan Doyle displays to the full his gift for narrative drive.

Having apparently killed off his celebrated sleuth in 1893, Conan Doyle found himself eight years later with a splendid idea for a novel of crime and suspense that cried out for Holmes, and he had the good sense to relent. Coming afresh to the task after a long break from Sherlock Holmes, Doyle produced what is probably one of the finest of all mystery novels, in spite of his feelings about Holmes. The story first appeared in nine monthly instalments in *The Strand Magazine* commencing in August 1901 and was a predictable success, although up against strong competition from H. G. Wells's *The First Men in the Moon*, appearing simultaneously in *The Strand* with disquieting illustrations by Claude Shepperson. But by the end of that first instalment Conan Doyle had made plain the futility of any competition with *this* story, and closed the episode with one of the greatest cliff-hanging lines of all serials – 'Mr Holmes, they were the footprints of a gigantic hound!'

Doyle freely acknowledged that he owed the idea for the story to Fletcher Robinson, who once regaled him with a legend of Dartmoor concerning a spectral hound. Immediately inspired, Doyle sketched out a plot and dashed off to Dartmoor with Robinson to pick up local details. The game was afoot once more, as readers were soon able to relish, to say nothing of dramatists, who eventually strove to find a means of transferring this strong drama to the stage and screen.

Of course, the grand climax, towards which the whole story is built, is the appearance of the Hound itself, its chase after Sir Henry Baskerville, and its final destruction by Holmes and Watson; all very difficult to enact, particularly upon the stage, as Ferdinand Bonn discovered when he first presented it at his Berliner Theater in 1907. He must have been asked so frequently how he staged it that he included a few notes in the text of the play:

> 'It so happened that I had a big, black dog that my wife was very attached to . . . when Argyll (the villain) disappears into the cave, the great black Hound springs over the stage in savage leaps, hunting him. The savage leaps were induced by a piece of wurst that my wife, standing in the wings, held up aloft tantalisingly.
>
> At first we put on the Hound a false head with electric lamps on, but it would have been loudly ridiculed; a little better was a muzzle with electric lamps. The limit of absurdity is always so much nearer when the audience attention is greater. The howling presented just as great difficulties. After trying with phonographs, automobile horns, steam whistles, and so on, we found the simplest and best way. A man howled through a gramophone horn, at a suitable distance.'

Although Ferdinand Bonn's play varied somewhat from Conan Doyle's original (Schloss Baskerville was in the Scottish Highlands, and Bonnie Prince Charlie's treasure was added to the property and title sought by the villain Stapleton, re-named Argyll), it preserved the essentials of the tale – the legend of a Hound destined to dispose of sundry members of the Baskerville family, and the use by the villain of the fears and superstitions created by the legend as a cover for a very material hound that he trains for his evil ends.

Bonn ran his two Sherlock Holmes plays in the repertoire of his theatre for a total of 351 performances, and on one auspicious evening *Der Hund* was given before the Kaiser himself.

In 1916 *The Hound* re-appeared on the stage in Spain as *La Tragedia de Baskerville*, by Gonzalo Jover and Enrique Arroyo. Once more the presentation of the Hound created problems, solved by a mechanical device:

> 'The dog, large and black, with red electric lights for eyes and another to indicate the tongue, is to be mounted on arched crossbows, with paws extended as though running. The crossbows are to be joined by two cross timbers, placed under the feet, and to the foremost cross piece a copper wire is to be attached in such fashion that it may be vigorously pulled, to give the animal a

galloping movement. Arrangement of the mechanical mounting is to be such that the appliances are not visible from the audience.'

The motion picture has great advantages over the stage in coping with these difficulties, for so much can be faked and simulated by skilful cutting, imaginative camera angles, and special effects.

On the screen the Hound was first unleashed in 1914 in *Der Hund von Baskerville*, written by Richard Oswald. It was a key film in his career, and thereafter his stature and reputation grew rapidly. His recognition of its importance to him was indicated years later, when he had his own thriving company, Richard Oswald-Film. In an advertisement for the company he showed miniature posters of all his successes, and the odd film out was the one not made by his company at all – *Der Hund*. It had been made by Vitascope, for whom Oswald then worked as a scenario writer, and it featured Alwin Neuss as Sherlock Holmes.

Despite the outbreak of the Great War, *Der Hund* was so well received that Vitascope went straight ahead with *Der Hund von Baskerville II*, which had the same director, writer and cast, but no Hound! The box-office pull of that title was so great in Germany that the string of sequels actually got to *Der Hund von Baskerville VI* before the nonsense ended. Needless to say, only the first film had been based on Conan Doyle's story, and, from the little information available, reasonably closely at that. This film was re-issued in 1919, and enjoyed a long life round the cinemas of Europe and the USA.

The next Hound out of the trap was in 1921 – a feature-length version by the English director Maurice Elvey that was part of the massive series of Sherlock Holmes films made by Stoll Picture Productions, with Eille Norwood as Sherlock Holmes. Like all the Stoll Holmes films, it was set in the early nineteen-twenties, but was a very faithful adaptation of the original. Maurice Elvey was an outstanding British director, and his firm control is apparent throughout this tautly dramatic piece. Against the calm underplaying of Eille Norwood was set a melodramatic Stapleton, played with great force by Lewis Gilbert. Cold and almost obsequious in the presence of Sherlock Holmes and Sir Henry Baskerville, Gilbert's Stapleton resents Sir Henry's attentions to his supposed sister Beryl Stapleton (really his wife), and when alone with her becomes a hard, enraged villain, railing at her in a truly terrifying manner, and on one occasion fetching her a blow in the mouth that made one really fear for the teeth of actress Betty Campbell.

As for the Hound, it made a worthy climax to the film. Probably for the only time on the screen, a real attempt was made to reproduce the appearance of the fearsome hound of hell described by Conan Doyle, and the flickering flames bursting from it were actually achieved by scratching them on the negative, frame by frame. The struggle with the Hound was staged largely in silhouette on the skyline, cleverly avoiding any tell-tale details of the arrangement.

STOLL FILM C° L™

THE HOUND OF THE BASKERVILLES

Baskerville Hall, 1921: Rex
McDougall (Sir Henry), Fred
Raynham (Barrymore), Hubert
Willis (Watson), and Eille
Norwood (Holmes)

Back in Germany, Richard Oswald had not forgotten the en-
thralling tale of the Hound, and returned to the subject in 1929
when he directed the last silent Sherlock Holmes film, *Der Hund
von Baskerville*. It may have been felt that another film with that
title would be a sure-fire winner in Germany, but unfortunately the
advent of talking pictures proved otherwise.

Carlyle Blackwell played Sherlock Holmes at the head of an
international cast, and although the adaptation was set in the 1920s
Blackwell's Holmes was equipped with the regulation deerstalker –
the only time it ever appeared in a Continental Holmes film, so far
as I can trace. The German approach to the subject was becoming
an expression of dark doings among the English aristocracy, and
the Hound tended to slip into the background as part of the sinister
Gothic atmosphere that the Teutonic mind believed to be ever
present in the castles of England.

Der Kinematograph commented that Fritz Rasp, as the villain
Stapleton, was playing the role for which he was born; this was a
careless remark about a distinguished and versatile character actor,
especially as he reappeared in a later film of *Der Hund* as Barrymore, the Baskerville's butler. With Rasp's Stapleton pitted against
Blackwell's Holmes, under Oswald's direction, the sheer weight of
experience surely must have produced a film of some quality.
Richard Oswald knew well the German liking for chiaroscuro and

Schloss Baskerville 1929

shadow; the romantic preoccupation with death, horror and nightmare, all of which can be found in this story. The influence of Max Reinhardt in staging and lighting can be seen in many of Oswald's films, and *Der Hund* is no exception. Oswald gave great weight to the disturbing aspects of the moor, the night-time, and interiors made uneasy with pools of darkness and light. That much we can tell from stills; perhaps one day we shall be able to get a print out of Russia, where the only copy is held, and see how well he brought it off.

Another missing Hound film, and the next chronologically, is the 1932 *The Hound of the Baskervilles*, chosen in a competition by readers of *Film Weekly* as the film they most wished to be made by Gainsborough Pictures at Islington. Very little is known of this second English Hound; true there was an interesting and lively account of the preparation and shooting in nine weekly magazine instalments, but apparently the finished product was not distinguished enough to merit lengthy criticism or indeed any detectable praise. On form and appearance Robert Rendel looks an unlikely choice as Sherlock Holmes, though he had the support of the excellent character actor Frederick Lloyd as Dr Watson. But the Hound was real, and enormous. Unfortunately the weekly *Diary of a Film*, which spends any amount of space on gossipy irrelevan-

Robert Rendel (Holmes) and Frederick Lloyd (Watson) in the first sound film of *The Hound of the Baskervilles* (Gainsborough 1932)

opposite: Georges Seroff (Watson) and Carlyle Blackwell searching for *Der Hund,* 1929

John Stuart (Sir Henry), learning never to act with animals, in the 1932 Gainsborough version

cies, tells us absolutely nothing about the Hound, which is, after all, the *raison d'être* of the whole piece, and which *Variety* considered the best actor of the lot, although even he 'bounded over rocks and walls like a big good-natured mongrel rather than a ferocious man-eater.' A great pity, because *there* was a golden opportunity, with the first sound version of *The Hound*, for some blood-curdling howling and snarling.

The third and final occasion that a German company invoked the Hound of Hell was in the troubled circumstances of Germany in 1937, when the Nazi hounds of hell were very close to being turned loose on Europe. The old favourite *Der Hund von Baskerville* proved to have great staying power during the ensuing war, and it is reported that a copy of the film was found in Hitler's private film library at Berchtesgaden.

This time there was no Richard Oswald in charge; though not yet departed for the USA, Oswald had made no films since 1933 and was not likely to in the Third Reich. So it fell to director Karl

86

Lamac to conjure up once again the macabre surroundings of Schloss Baskerville and its demoniac dog, and while the beast and the buildings may have been more or less according to Doyle, the late nineteen-thirties characters were totally inappropriate. Bruno Güttner as Holmes, with a flat cap, polo-neck jersey, leather overcoat and an automatic pistol, was straight out of Edgar Wallace.

We come at last to the most satisfying version of *The Hound of the Baskervilles*, and arguably the best Sherlock Holmes film to be made. In 1939 Twentieth Century–Fox made the first American-produced *Hound*, with a resounding success that ensured a prompt sequel. The adaptation was superbly carried out, and the casting was exemplary. The film marked the teaming together of Basil Rathbone and Nigel Bruce as Sherlock Holmes and Dr Watson, roles they continued playing on the screen and the radio for another seven years. But they were never to achieve again the brilliance of the performances they gave in *The Hound*; nor did they ever have any other comparable vehicles for their portrayals.

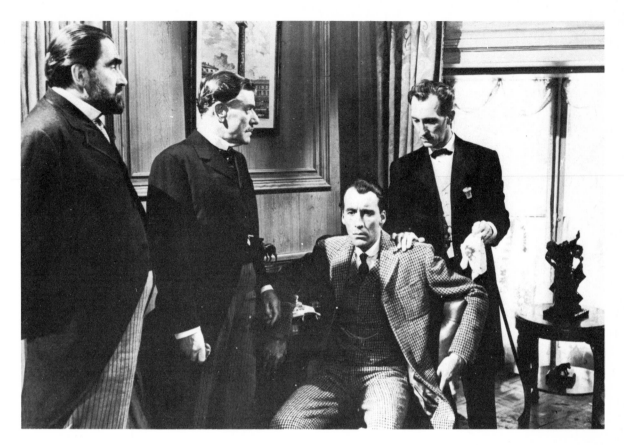

Certainly there were some deviations from the Conan Doyle tale, but nothing of great consequence; the intelligently written dialogue took careful recognition of the Holmesian traditions, and the settings were meticulously prepared, for here was the first Sherlock Holmes film placed in the proper Victorian context, which recovered so much of the eerie atmosphere of Doyle's original. The grim, fog-laden moor was created indoors at the Fox studios, and was excitingly used to the utmost in the chase and attack of Sir Henry by the Hound. Spectacularly staged, the scene remains one of the great gripping climaxes of the screen.

Twenty years after the grand climax came the great anti-climax, when Hammer Films presented the first coloured cur. Renowned for their explicitly bloody horror films, including various new series with Frankenstein and Dracula, their Sherlock Holmes film was heralded as a Horror Hound, and the cast included many regular Hammer players, in particular Peter Cushing as Holmes. The writers tampered unnecessarily with the original and dragged in various absurd features – a tarantula spider, a ruined Abbey with a sacrificial slab, corpse mutilation, a webbed hand on Sir Hugo and on Stapleton – that had no basis whatsoever in the novel. The finished product proved to be neither a good adaptation nor a whole-hearted horror movie. It was very disappointingly made, and the eventual appearance of the Hound thrilled no one.

Nothing to do with the original story, Christopher Lee (Sir Henry) recovers from a nasty encounter with a giant spider (Hammer 1959)

opposite, top: Schloss Baskerville 1937, with Bruno Güttner, Peter Voss (*Lord* Henry, no less) and Fritz Odemar (Watson)

opposite, bottom: The spirit and flavour of Paget, *The Strand,* late Victorian England and the whole Holmes genre are evoked in this still of Rathbone and Bruce (Twentieth Century–Fox 1939)

Also nothing to do with the original story, Marla Landi (Cecile Stapleton) perishes in explicit Hammer style

Christopher Lee revealed some of the risks involved in appearing as the target for the hound:

'Conan Doyle's Henry Baskerville was a rather unimaginative, rather rude, rough-edged Colonial . . . they decided to play him as a romantic lead in my case, which I think was valuable in the context, because if you put somebody on the screen who really *is* like that, people are going to find him dull and a bore . . . The most unconvincing thing about *The Hound of the Baskervilles* was the dog, which is, of course, inevitably a great problem . . . They got a young Great Dane, took him to the studios, and got him accustomed to the people and the lights and the heat and the noise, which he eventually did. When the time came to shoot, when he had to go into action and attack me, he wouldn't. So they had to irritate him, to the point where he got so annoyed and so irritated that he *did* go for me . . . I had to protect my face and neck from his attack. The dog really was worked up!'

opposite: BBC Television's docile doggie, 1968

It seems extraordinary that, with Christopher Lee available, he was cast as Henry Baskerville and not Sherlock Holmes. The actor

90

who would have made a good Stapleton, and who actually played Sherlock Holmes in this sad spectacle, Peter Cushing, reappeared in an easily forgettable series of television plays transmitted by the BBC in 1968, during which *The Hound* was given in two parts. Once again there was needless tampering with the story. One is ever amazed at the crassness of writers and producers who insist on trying to 'improve' first-class stories. In this instance the whole mystery of the spectral nature of the hound was destroyed by the stupid addition of an incident in which *Watson* is chased by a hound that leaves very material scratches on the woodwork, long before the Hound's hunting of Sir Henry Baskerville. And when *that* climax came it was without either a build-up or a release of tension. Regrettably, such inept production was all too typical. In a series that was

Baskerville Hall 1971, at Perth Repertory Theatre. Richard Simpson (Watson) and Tim Preece

opposite: More studio mire in ABC Television's 1972 version. Bernard Fox (Watson) and Stewart Granger

noticeably lacking in humour, there was a visual joke in the stained glass windows of the BBC's Baskerville Hall, where the motto 'Cave Canem Nocte' appeared. It means 'Beware of the dog in the night-time' and I wonder if it was intended. The joke is that the reference to a dog in the night-time comes from a different Sherlock Holmes story altogether.

But if the Hammer film and the BBC teleplay of *The Hound* were poor, the film version made in the USA in 1972, specifically for television, can only be described as a disaster. Stewart Granger was featured as Sherlock Holmes in a production that looked and sounded like a B-picture made in the worst years of Poverty Row.

Without wasting space on a catalogue of all the blunders and changes, one need only point to the great lack of a Hound in the plot. Apart from the Baskerville curse sequence at the beginning, there was no mounting fear or suspicion of a Hound, no mysterious baying over the moors, no Hound chasing Seldon the convict – in fact, none of the off-stage menace of the Hound that in the book builds up to the dramatic emergence of the beast and its pursuit of Sir Henry Baskerville. In this absurd film the Hound doesn't even attack Sir Henry: it attacks Holmes!

The kindest thing that television stations could have done for their viewers would have been to transmit, instead, the 1939 film of *The Hound*, with Rathbone and Bruce. The only complaint the viewers might have had would have been lack of colour. That dubious need apart, the 1939 version of this most filmed story of the Holmes saga is likely to hold the trophy for many years to come.

'My Friend and Colleague'

If Conan Doyle had really meant business when he attempted to get rid of Sherlock Holmes, he should have killed off Dr Watson. That's the key to it. Without Watson there really can be no Holmes.

Holmes without Watson has become unthinkable. It is Watson's handling of his narrative, and his function as a buffer between Sherlock Holmes and the world of ordinary mortals that is so valuable. Clearly both characters are projections of different facets of Arthur Conan Doyle's personality, and he deployed his literary skills with great shrewdness to separate and contrast the two individuals. The stolid, level-headed, practical good sense of Dr Watson was deliberately contrived to offset the overpowering and at times seemingly unnatural brilliance of Sherlock Holmes.

Since an author cannot persist in subjecting us to monologues by the hero in which he extols his own mental virtuosity, a secondary character to whom it can all be expounded becomes essential. As a literary device that was no new idea, but Conan Doyle developed it to an extraordinary degree. Sherlock Holmes is always the man of marvels, amazing us by his supremacy over other persons concerned in unravelling the mystery, and we stand beside Watson in awe and wonder when Holmes finally condescends to enlighten us.

Of course, the constant repetition of this process can become boring, and Doyle cleverly varied the complexity of the puzzles and the degree of obscurity so that, while we recognised that Holmes had worked out *all* the answers, we were able to arrive at a few, *before* they were explained to poor bewildered Watson.

Regrettably this aspect of the Holmes–Watson partnership has been taken to absurd limits by successive dramatists and directors, and Watson has been reduced to the level of bumbling comic relief. Not only is that wrong for Watson but it diminishes the stature of Holmes. The whole purpose of Dr Watson, as created by Conan Doyle, is to provide a foil of reasonable intelligence (after all, he *was* an Army doctor) to contrast with the super-intelligence of Holmes, and to soften the less-attractive features of such a character for us. For this to succeed, Watson has to be a person one can visualise sharing lodgings with Holmes over many years. He must be able to tolerate Holmes, with all his idiosyncrasies, and *be* tolerable to Holmes.

Unfortunately very few dramatists have been able to appreciate the difficulty of using the character of Watson, once his functions of narrator and interpreter have been removed. Consequently they have relegated him to a minor position in the drama, when they have included him at all.

Certainly some early stage pieces and many early films had no Dr Watson to accompany Sherlock Holmes. Paradoxically, a couple of early foreign films filched him to support *their* respective heroes: both Germany's *Stuart Keen* (1913) and Denmark's *Dr Gar el Harma* (1913) had a Dr Watson.

In the first stage drama, Charles Rogers's *Sherlock Holmes* (1893), Dr Watson actually played a major part – as the kidnapped victim of a homicidal maniac. In all seriousness, the dramatist wrote into his plot a Mrs Watson, who berates Holmes for not immediately tracing her husband, because she believes Holmes is still in love with her!

In Gillette's *Sherlock Holmes*, Watson was largely a nonentity, subordinated to the starring role which Gillette had devised for himself; but in Doyle's *The Speckled Band*, Watson plays a very large part in establishing the opening situation of the plot. He is present at Stoke Moran Manor as a friend of the stepdaughters of the villain, Dr Roylott, and he has to make some important observations and deductions because Holmes does not appear until halfway through the play. When he does, he asks Watson to refresh his memory about the mysterious death of one of the stepdaughters: 'An inquest was it not, with a string of most stupid and ineffectual witnesses?' to which Watson responds, with deflating mildness, 'I was one of them.'

Although the tale had become unbalanced in its translation from short story to play, it contained a very satisfactory handling of Watson, whereas subsequent stage treatments tended to be of the usual doormat and puppy-dog varieties.

On the silent screen the first identifiable Watson was Hubert Willis in the vast Stoll series, but he was largely identifiable in name only. True, he went through the motions pretty well as described by Doyle in the stories, but he was such a colourless character, in appearance as well as performance, that he probably qualifies as the most undistinguished of all Watsons, as least in films.

At the same time as Willis, another British actor, Roland Young, played Watson opposite John Barrymore's Holmes, obviously with less restraint than Willis. Barrymore's comment on Young's portrayal was that the 'quiet, agreeable bastard had stolen, not one, but every damned scene!' It was a typical Barrymore exaggeration: Young was a good Watson who did not detract from Holmes at all.

The first Watson in talking pictures was H. Reeves Smith, comparatively elderly looking against the Holmes of Clive Brook – but then he was saddled with a grown-up daughter, Mary, whose imminent marriage arrangements were the starting-point for a complicated shipboard mystery involving both Moriarty and Moran. Watson's part in all this, apart from being father of the bride-to-be, was a reasonable one, even though the characterisation leaned towards the fatuous. Much more fatuous was Clive Brook's other

Clive Brook contemplates Watson with a daughter (H. Reeves Smith and Betty Lawford) in *The Return of Sherlock Holmes* (Paramount 1929)

Watson, Reginald Owen, who was barely in the film at all, and no sort of relationship between the two men was remotely conceivable.

Ian Fleming, a character actor with a long career in British films, was another Watson that Holmes would have found exceedingly sponge-like. Inoffensive and self-effacing, he contributed little to the partnership, but at least did not get in the way of Arthur Wontner's splendid Holmes. Fleming was replaced in the middle of the series of Wontner films by Ian Hunter, on the grounds that a more romantic actor was necessary for *The Sign of Four* (the same fate had befallen Hubert Willis with the silent film of the same story ten years earlier). For the two remaining Wontner films, Ian Fleming returned as Watson and everyone behaved as though the lapse into love interest had never occurred. In fact it has only reappeared once since then.

Fritz Odemar and Heinz Rühmann followed as unlikely Watsons in two German films of 1937. Odemar, like his Holmes, Bruno Güttner, looked extremely Continental and was very much out of his depth. Rühmann, a celebrated character actor, was an unrecognisable Watson in an incomprehensible film, *Der Mann, der Sherlock Holmes war*. Wrote Graham Greene:

The fuddy-duddy of them all: Nigel Bruce 'helping' Sir Ronald Ramsgate. Keeper of the Crown Jewels (Henry Stephenson) to guard the famous jewel, the Star of Delhi, in *The Adventures of Sherlock Holmes* (Twentieth Century–Fox 1939). Little do they know that the clean-shaven policeman listening in is Moriarty himself! (George Zucco)

'I happened to see it in Mexico, and still wonder what they made of it, those dubious *mestizos* in the cheap seats, made of the two crooks who, posing in a German spa as Holmes and Watson, were always encountering an enigmatic man in a deerstalker and a cape given to fits of hearty Teutonic laughter in hotel lounges whenever he caught sight of them.'

Without doubt the best-remembered Dr Watson, and one of the worst-conceived, was that of Nigel Bruce, who had the misfortune to portray a version of the character that has been called 'Boobus Britannicus'. That was not Nigel Bruce's fault. His acting was generally limited to playing rather inflexible upper-class British gentlemen, and during his career in Hollywood he gave scores of excellent performances in that type of part. But as Watson he was obliged to enact an old duffer whose mental level at times was about that of a small child.

In the first two films of the Basil Rathbone–Nigel Bruce partnership, set in the correct Victorian period, this was not over-emphasised, although even then the idea was apparent. But when Universal produced the Holmes and Watson of the 1940s, the usage of Watson verged on the grotesque. Basil Rathbone's Sherlock

Colin Blakely, with Irene Handl as Mrs. Hudson (*Mirisch 1970*)

Holmes aged a little from the smart-looking sleuth with patent-leather hair, seen in *The Hound of the Baskervilles*, but by comparison Nigel Bruce's Dr Watson grew almost senile. Embarrassed or humiliated by Holmes, he would withdraw, grumbling ''Strordinary thing, mumble, mumble . . . 'strordinary thing'. It was a very sad spectacle, especially as those Universal films had an extended life on television in the 1950s and 1960s, so that generations have grown up believing Watson always to be a dunderhead. It was unfortunate because basically Rathbone and Bruce made an ideal combination. One has only to see again their performances in the 1939 *The Hound* to be reminded of that. Extraordinary thing indeed.

One is forced to admit that the handling of Nigel Bruce made him the first *memorable* Dr Watson, and later actors of the part still recall Bruce's impersonation when discussing their own work in the role. Peter Sallis for instance, who was in *Baker Street*:

'I was in a musical in London in 1963 called *She Loves Me*, and I worked with Hal Prince, who later directed *Baker Street*. He asked me if I would be interested in playing Dr Watson and of course I was. Not very long after *She Loves Me* closed I got the formal offer . . . Watson wasn't a very big part; he didn't feature as much in the musical as he has done in films, when Nigel Bruce made a big name for himself doing that, amongst other things. It was a relatively small part and I had one nice number in it. I think I was reasonably right casting for the part, but to start off with a musical on Broadway – I couldn't believe it, it was so exciting . . . I was in it for something like six months and then I left to appear in something else, but I enjoyed being in it enormously.'

Raymond Francis was Dr Watson to Alan Wheatley's Holmes in the 1951 BBC television series. He mentioned Nigel Bruce as well:

'I'd seen films, mostly Hollywood films, with Basil Rathbone and Nigel Bruce, and I always thought it was a pity that Watson was made to look a bit of a buffoon, and sometimes *quite* a buffoon, which I don't think really added up. It's fine if you want to get a laugh, but it's a cheap laugh . . . After all, Watson has a certain history . . . He might find it a little difficult to keep up with Holmes's very quick brain, but that doesn't make him a foolish man. Fortunately Lejeune wrote it on the lines that he wasn't completely nonplussed, and my Watson was always *in* the situation, but obviously a little adrift from the quick, quick thinking of Holmes.'

The Dr Watson in *The Private Life of Sherlock Holmes* was Colin Blakely, who also referred to Bruce:

'Billy Wilder asked for me through Bob Stephens in fact, because we had worked together a lot in the theatre, and he wanted two people who knew each other's work well. That's the main reason he chose me . . . There's got to be a certain ease between Holmes and Watson, and he wanted them to be played slightly younger than they had been before. He changed Watson from the Nigel Bruce characterization because he wanted Watson to be impressionable and eager and more youthful. He wasn't a stupid man, or dense, but he was just so eager. Compared with Sherlock Holmes anybody was outclassed.'

In the 1965 television series Nigel Stock began as Watson to Douglas Wilmer's Holmes, and continued with Peter Cushing in the subsequent 1968 series. His was an attractive portrayal at which he worked very hard to avoid the earlier bumbling interpretations, and he was able to convey a credible friendship existing between these two diverse, yet complementary, characters. In the second sequence he was faced with appearing in *The Sign of Four*, with its romance between Watson and Mary Morstan. The adaptation was handled very carefully, and changed so that Watson does *not* get the girl in the end. Thus the series was not disturbed by having Watson married, and this particular episode ended on a thoughtful, subdued note that enabled Stock to strengthen and deepen his penetration of the character. Douglas Wilmer commented:

Nigel Stock has been Watson to three Holmeses: Douglas Wilmer and Peter Cushing on television, and Robert Hardy on record (*BBC television 1968*)

Anthony Quayle (Dr Murray) and Judi Dench (Sally) have to cope with the deliberately blundering Watson of Donald Houston in *A Study in Terror* (Compton – Sir Nigel 1965)

'It's very difficult to know what to do with Watson. People complain that he's reduced to a sort of ass who stood around and made Holmes look brilliant by saying "Goodness me!", but it reduces Holmes by his very stupidity . . . It is not *enough* to have Watson just coming on and saying "My goodness. How extraordinary, Holmes. How brilliant you are, and I don't know how you do it, Holmes". In the books he's the person that leads you through the labyrinth of Holmes's mind. This is what I feel to be the principal difficulty of dramatisations. There are not the softening comments of Watson. There is not the buffer between the audience and Holmes, nor the affectionate understanding of Watson. This is the *function* of Watson. Otherwise he's got no function but to stand there as just a straight man, a buffoon.'

A Study in Terror (1965) contained one of the most likeable Watsons of all – Donald Houston. Throughout the film he appeared to be enjoying his role, and the result was a robust, good-humoured companionship between the two men. When Holmes required him to make a nuisance of himself, he did so at great personal embarrassment but full of determination not to let his colleague down. It was a refreshing performance, far removed from the customary stooge.

Regrettably, the Nigel Bruce portrayal has influenced succeeding directors and writers to a considerable degree, and in 1974 the concept was pushed to the ultimate in Matthew Lang's play *Sherlock's Last Case*. The theatre programme stated that the author had never read the Conan Doyle stories when he wrote the play; his knowledge of Sherlock Holmes was derived from the Rathbone–Bruce films. The treatment was forseeable to a large extent: an arrogant, overbearing Holmes and a servile, long-suffering Watson, both greatly exaggerated. The twist came in the final scene, when the worm turns. Poor downtrodden Watson discloses that he is the instigator of the entire mystery they have become involved in, with the sole purpose of freeing himself from his subservience by doing away with Holmes. This he proceeds to do as the final blackout takes place. Peter Bayliss played this difficult part extremely well, presenting at the end a demented doctor driven to the final resort of destroying the cause of his madness.

No other Dr Watson has been made such a tragicomic figure; a few have been merely pathetic, and some have been allowed to perform as acceptable and believable characters, but these seem to have been rare. One that came near to it was Edward Fox in *Dr Watson and the Darkwater Hall Mystery*, an audacious piece written by Kingsley Amis for BBC Television, in which Watson saw Holmes off on a rest cure and immediately became involved in a country-house shooting-party mystery. The triviality of the plot, encumbered with red herrings and excessive attention to Watson's amorous propensities, made it even more difficult for Edward Fox to convey the idea of Watson without Holmes. Using Holmesian methods and Watsonian courage he solved the crime, but one was left with the

Without the moustache Edward Fox would make a good Holmes. In fact, he is Watson in *Dr Watson and the Darkwater Hall Mystery* (BBC Television 1974). Written by Kingsley Amis, the story omits Holmes altogether

feeling that it may have been largely good luck; and as the play finished with Watson preparing to deal with another client announced by Mrs Hudson, it seemed high time that the Master was back.

Holmes and Watson are, after all, inseparable, as even Holmes himself eventually had to acknowledge (albeit tongue-in-cheek) in *The Blanched Soldier*:

'If I burden myself with a companion in my various little enquiries it is not done out of sentiment or caprice, but it is that Watson has some remarkable characteristics of his own, to which in his modesty he has given small attention amid his exaggerated estimates of my own performances. A confederate who forsees your conclusions and course of action is always dangerous, but one to whom each development comes as a perpetual surprise, and to whom the future is always a closed book, is, indeed, an ideal helpmate.'

Paul Daneman as Dr Watson,
Birmingham Repertory Theatre,
1954 (*Lisel Haas*)

Howard Marion Crawford on
location in England, 1954

opposite: Andre Morell, a first-class
Watson, had too little chance to
shine in *The Hound* (Hammer 1959)

The Master of Disguise

'The stage lost a fine actor', Dr Watson says of Sherlock Holmes, 'when he became a specialist in crime.' In fact those great talents were not wholly wasted, although the unsuspecting public (both honest and criminal) were seldom aware of them. Holmes's histrionic abilities were the means of concluding many successful cases.

Of course, Watson was almost always deceived. For all his experience of Holmes and his ways, he still thought in *The Final Problem* when they were avoiding Moriarty, that the venerable Italian priest was a blundering intruder into their reserved compartment, and not until the train drew out was he enlightened.

On the other hand, Watson can be forgiven for not seeing through the elderly deformed bookseller who followed him home in *The Empty House*; after all, he believed Holmes to have been dead for some years, and was completely unprepared for such a shock.

Even though Count Negretto Sylvius detected that he was being followed, he did not penetrate Holmes's disguise, and even picked up the old lady's parasol for her. Naturally Irene Adler was different. She not only tumbled to Holmes and his tricks, but practised the same upon him. But we must own that she was exceptional among the many who came into contact with the great man.

The stories contain many references to Holmes's fondness for disguises and love of theatrical effects, and dramatists have not been slow to use this characteristic to best advantage. Actors, too, have seized the opportunity to give a sort of virtuoso cadenza within their main role: a character sketch to show off their versatility and to give them a little relief from playing the rather unvarying part of Holmes.

Even the earliest stage plays incorporated this attractive feature of the character. In Charles Rogers's play *Sherlock Holmes* (1894) it was a simple disguise as a tailor to enable Holmes to escape from jail, but in *The Bank of England* (1900) Holmes had a fine old time, appearing as an old gentleman from India, the captain of the Bank guard and finally as the ghost of a murdered forger.

William Gillette's play *Sherlock Holmes* (1899) was partly based on the story *A Scandal in Bohemia* and understandably Gillette utilised the ruse of the old clergyman hurt in a cab accident to excellent effect, but no photographs seem to be available of that part of Gillette's portrayal. In Doyle's play *The Speckled Band*, Holmes turns up as a gas-fitter and insults the waiting Watson

Sherlock Holmes (Georges
Treville) posing as Juanes Rilto,
'a foreigner of good position', in
The Speckled Band (Eclair 1913)

before revealing himself. Conan Doyle again wrote an elaborate old woman disguise for Holmes into his one-act play *The Crown Diamond*, but removed all but the Count's reference to it when he converted the play into the short story *The Mazarin Stone.*

On the screen the outstanding disguise specialist was Eille Norwood, who was such a master of make-up himself that remarkable disguises were made a feature of most of his forty-seven Holmes films, even when they did not figure in the original stories. At the same time as Norwood there was a noteworthy cameo by John Barrymore. His film was largely based on the Gillette play, and he too appeared as the old clergyman, removing his make-up piece by piece as the scene continued. (When John Wood did it at the Aldwych, the surprise was achieved by removing his disguise in one bold stroke.)

Clive Brook had two disguises in each of his two sound films (if you count donning a welder's mask as one of them), but none of them were effective from the audience's point of view. Later in the 1930s Arthur Wontner achieved several extremely clever characterisations, particularly in *The Sign of Four*, and after him Basil Rathbone appeared in two splendid little sketches in his first two Holmes

opposite: Eille Norwood again. Here Holmes is disguised as Colonel Moran's German servant in the stage play *The Return of Sherlock Holmes* (1923)

films for Fox. Later, when Rathbone appeared in the Universal series, the disguises were rarely so good; on one occasion a Holmes disguise is used merely to set up Watson (who later accosts a total stranger resembling the disguise) so that he can be embarrassed. Such was the treatment of Watson in that series.

Certainly the dramatic emergence of Holmes from behind an impenetrable disguise is often a source of comedy for the dramatists. One can always be sure that poor old Watson will be discomfited by the sudden revelation that he has been deceived by Holmes yet again. It is never explained why Watson hardly ever sees the preparation of these masterpieces of make-up, which surely must have taken long periods of making ready to be so convincing.

Just occasionally it is obvious who it must be, even to Watson:

'Accustomed as I was to my friend's amazing powers of disguises, I had to look three times before I was certain that it was indeed he.'

The 'amiable and simple-minded Nonconformist clergyman' of *A Scandal in Bohemia*. Eille Norwood (Holmes) and Joan Beverley (Irene Adler)

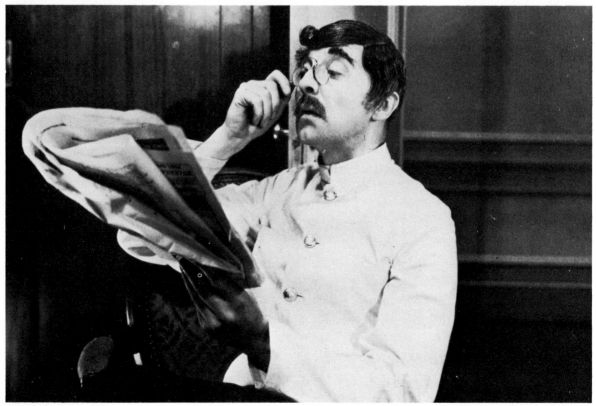

Ho...

opposite: On board an ocean liner in *The Return of Sherlock Holmes* (Paramount 1929), Clive Brook is disguised as a musician in the ship's orchestra . . .

. . . and later as a cabin steward

'It's so obviously me,' said Clive Brook of this disguise in *Sherlock Holmes* (Fox 1932)

A frame enlargement from *The Hound of the Baskervilles* (Twentieth Century–Fox 1939) shows Basil Rathbone's excellent peddler disguise

Basil Rathbone and Gale Sondergaard in *Spider Woman* (Universal 1944)

'Those seaman disguises were meant to be seen through', said Ronald Howard. He is on the right, Howard Marion Crawford on the left (Guild Films 1954)

Another seaman: Christopher Lee

One of the few really good
disguises in recent years was John
Neville's in *A Study in Terror*
(Compton, Sir Nigel 1965)

Furnished Rooms to Let

One of Arthur Conan Doyle's strokes of genius was to establish the Holmes and Watson partnership in a real locality. Baker Street, already well-known for its association with Madame Tussaud's wax-works, is now even better-known as the location of the rooms in Mrs Hudson's house that were occupied by Marylebone's most famous inhabitants. That is no exaggeration, as was apparent in 1951 when the St Marylebone Borough Council staged the Sherlock Holmes Exhibition, in Baker Street of course, as their contribution to the Festival of Britain.

Although Doyle picked an actual location, he wisely gave the house a fictitious number, and there never was a 221B under any of the numbering systems in Baker Street or Upper Baker Street. Needless to say, that has not prevented Holmesian scholars from constructing elaborate theories as to which real house in Baker Street *could* have been 221B and what the layout of the celebrated rooms was like. The references in the stories to various features of the lodgings provide only limited data, but there is sufficient information, coupled with the known general style of Baker Street houses, for a good attempt at the consulting-room or general living room of Holmes and Watson.

Face to face: Emil Helsengreen (Moriarty) and Dorph-Petersen, Denmark 1902

An austere setting of the consulting room in *A Study in Scarlet* (Samuelson 1914). Watson unknown; Fred Paul (old woman) and James Bragington (Holmes)

In *The Final Problem* (Stoll 1923), Percy Standing (Moriarty) delivers his parting threats to Hubert Willis and Eille Norwood in their interesting 1920s room

opposite, top: That confrontation again – Justus Hagman and Knut Nyblom, Sweden 1902

opposite, bottom: The first film version of the same scene, in *Sherlock Holmes* (Nordisk 1908). The crude, ruffianly Moriarty is unknown; Edith Plio was 'Billy' and Viggo Larsen was Holmes. Not a bad attempt at Baker Street for its time

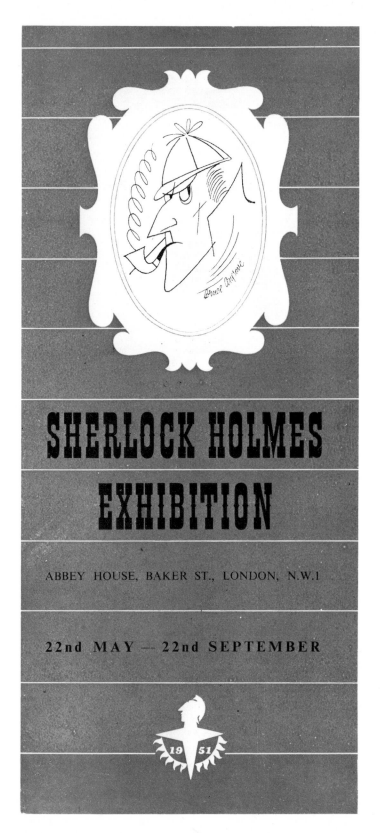

SHERLOCK HOLMES
EXHIBITION

ABBEY HOUSE, BAKER ST., LONDON, N.W.1

22nd MAY — 22nd SEPTEMBER

opposite, top: Eille Norwood's Baker Street room on the stage (1923) looks a little shabby compared with the film set. H. G. Stoker (Watson) holds Lauderdale Maitland (Col Moran)

opposite, bottom: 'Motor transportation more than anything else is responsible for the frightful increase in crime,' says Clive Brook in Sherlock Holmes (Fox 1932), and demonstrates his electro-magnetic ray for stopping getaway cars to his fiancée Alice Faulkner (Miriam Jordan), watched by Billy (Howard Leeds). This Fox conception of the Baker Street Room looks more like something at Universal, left over from a Frankenstein movie

Festival of Britain leaflet, 1951

opposite: the patriotic vandalism of Sherlock Holmes, who shot the initials VR into the wall, can be seen just to the left of the door. Michael Weight made sure that every single item of bric-a-brac mentioned in the stories could be found somewhere

The stage designer Michael Weight carried out a fascinating reconstruction of this room for the 1951 exhibition. The remainder of the exhibition consisted of exhibits in glass cases, illustrations, displays of books and so on, but the Baker Street room was the principal attraction of the show. It was affectionately adorned with the *bric-à-brac* of a late Victorian interior, and the clutter of the untidy hoarder that was Sherlock Holmes.

The entire Holmesian canon had been combed for details casually referred to by Doyle, who in fact mentioned many more things in the room than one at first realises. The jack-knife spiking letters to the mantelpiece, the Persian slipper full of tobacco, and the cigars in the coal scuttle are easy ones, inserted to colour the character of Holmes rather than describe the room. Less obvious were many of the things Holmes and Watson are mentioned as using, and which must therefore have been parked somewhere round the room – such things as walking sticks, riding crop, magnifying lens, reference books (Whittaker's, Bradshaw, *Who's Who* and Holmes' own index volumes).

In the story *The Cardboard Box* Holmes plays his remarkable mind reading trick on Watson, then explains the train of deduction by which he broke in on Watson's thoughts with an appropriate observation (a trick he scorns when Dupin does it). From his explanation we learn, in passing, that the room contains a framed portrait of General Gordon and an unframed one of Henry Ward Beecher.

Highlight of the 1951 Sherlock Holmes Exhibition was Michael Weight's grand reconstruction of the room, complete with sounds of horse-drawn vehicles, street musicians, vendors and barrel-organ, all issuing from beyond the fog-begrimed windows

SHERLOCK HOLMES EXHIBITION, LONDON, 1951
LIVING ROOM, 221 B, BAKER ST., RECONSTRUCTED BY MICHAEL WEIGHT

The Baker Street Room at the
Château de Lucens, Switzerland,
established by Adrian Conan
Doyle and now alas disappeared

By inference one can expect to see there the cabinet photograph of *the* woman, Irene Adler, that Holmes chose as his reward from the King of Bohemia; the dried skin of the deadly snake known as *The Speckled Band* (and a poker that has been bent and straightened, from the same story); boxing gloves ('You might have aimed high, if you had joined the fancy', the prizefighter McMurdo told Holmes in *The Sign of Four*).

Everything of this nature was skilfully incorporated into the realistic room by Michael Weight, who added some delightful touches wholly in keeping with the subject, which justly aroused admiration. There were fresh crumpets on the table, renewed daily (a natural for facetious press comments), and from beyond the fog-begrimed windows came a continuous succession of Victorian street sounds – an itinerant musician, horses and carriages, street vendors, a barrel organ and so on.

This was the first really detailed representation of the room based on textual references, and since then film-set and stage designers have often taken it as a model for their settings. Shortly after the exhibition closed, BBC television presented a six-part series of Sherlock Holmes adventures in which the Baker Street set surpassed even the exhibition room with a wealth of gorgeous realistic details, all scrupulously relevant to the period or to the stories.

Before 1951 the endeavours had been extremely variable, ranging from the perfunctory to the extraordinary; from the dreary, ordinary sitting-room to the lair of the mad scientist.

Even so, some efforts were made to present a room that the remarkable Holmes would have occupied. The William Gillette stage play showed a reasonably conventional Victorian room, described in the stage directions as 'An open, cheerful room, but not too much decorated . . . Books, music, violins, tobacco pouches, pipes, tobacco, etc., are scattered about the room with some disorder. Various odd things are hung about . . . The room gives more an impression of an artist's studio'. The detailed scene plot went to some lengths to emphasise the amount and type of litter and paraphernalia adorning the room, which seems a little at variance with the dignified Holmes that Gillette portrayed.

Productions of the play tended to follow the lines of this plan, especially as it was designed to suit the elaborate stage business carefully written into the directions by Gillette.

Conan Doyle's own play *The Speckled Band* could have been expected to contain *the* authentic depiction of the Baker Street room, but Doyle was never interested in that kind of scholarship. When he wrote his stories he decked them with just sufficient trimmings to colour the background and establish the settings. All these were secondary to the forceful flow of his narrative, and he had no intention of creating what he unconsciously achieved – the atmospheric depiction of a late-Victorian world that has now become a large part of the attraction of the Sherlock Holmes ethos. So when he adapted his own short story for the stage under financial necessity, he gave no more attention to the setting than dramatic purposes required. There was no description, at the beginning of the scene, of the general effect to be attained, as was the case with the Gillette play, but the props list includes such well-remembered items as the Persian slipper hanging by the fireplace; clay pipes in the coal scuttle; newspapers scattered over the floor, and so on. Conan Doyle had done *some* homework.

In both the Gillette play and *The Speckled Band* the scenes in Baker Street were relatively small, and the sets could not be made too complex both for reasons of scene changing and because the productions were also intended to go on tour. Similarly, in the early years of the movies, elaborate interior sets could seldom be afforded; neither could they be justified because of the time they consumed in a period when film making was measured in days rather than weeks. Consequently a lot of the properties and furnishings were painted on backdrops, and many sets were simply modified from film to film to save time and money. Even so, some attempts were made to show room interiors that reflected the life style of an intellectual.

Later, as film budgets expanded, more ambitious settings were attempted, as can be seen in some of the accompanying illustrations, with varying degrees of success, and similarly the exteriors of Baker Street have only been attempted comparatively recently, the finest being the magnificent set specially built at Pinewood Studios for *The Private Life of Sherlock Holmes*. In the mutilated form in which the film was finally released we only saw such brief glimpses of this sumptuous set that they could almost have got away with painted scenery again.

The focal point of the famous
room, as created for the series of
TV films made by Guild Films in
1954

'You can see the meticulous
trouble that producer Ian Atkins
took with the sets,' said Alan
Wheatley (BBC Television 1951)

Considerable care was taken with
the Guild Films Baker Street set;
after all, it was needed for a series
of 39 adventures. Here it comes to
life, with a relaxed-looking Ronald
Howard and Howard Marion
Crawford in conversation with
Ivan Desny

The 'chemistry corner' of the Guild Films set

Baker Street in the Constantin Film Studios (Berlin 1962), with Christopher Lee and Thorley Walters

GOLDEN ERA
present
"SHERLOCK HOLMES
AND THE
DEADLY NECKLACE"
'U'
starring
CHRISTOPHER LEE · SENTA BERGER
and THORLEY WALTERS

A Study in Terror (Compton— Sir Nigel, 1965) had a lovingly re-created Baker Street set at Shepperton. Robert Morley (Mycroft Holmes) and John Neville (Sherlock) wait while Donald Houston (Watson) talks to the Director, James Hill

In strong contrast with the minute detail achieved in other Holmesian productions, the settings for the musical *Baker Street* (1965) seemed rather crudely executed. Here Martin Gabel (Moriarty) gloats over Fritz Weaver (Holmes) and Peter Sallis (Watson)

The Colchester Repertory Theatre
had a very economical set for
*Sherlock Holmes and the Speckled
Band* (1968). Clive Rust as
Watson and Roger Heathcott as
Holmes

Designer Alex Trauner made the
Baker Street interiors rather
palatial for *The Private Life of
Sherlock Holmes* with Robert
Stephens and Colin Blakely
(Mirisch 1970)

In a rare animated cartoon depiction of Holmes and Watson the Baker Street background had to reflect the super-efficient Sherlock Holmes in an instructional film for the Electricity Council, *The Case of the Metal-Sheathed Elements* (Larkins Studio 1972)

Also palatial was the set in ABC Television's *The Hound of the Baskervilles* (1972)

The outside of Baker Street is, with one exception, never seen on the stage, and very infrequently on the screen. Here Sidney Seaward (Colonel Moran) prepares to shoot across the street at what he believes is a real detective. *The Empty House* (Stoll 1921)

opposite, top: Back to *that* play, same setting, same positions, at the Aldwych Theatre, London, in 1974. Philip Locke and John Wood

opposite, bottom: 221B became a splendid town residence in *The Adventures of Sherlock Holmes* (Twentieth Century–Fox 1939). The hansom driver (Arthur Hohl) is really one of Moriarty's men eavesdropping on Sir Robert Ramsgate (Henry Stephenson) and Ann Brandon (Ida Lupino). The postman is evidently puzzled as to how to get the letter through the door

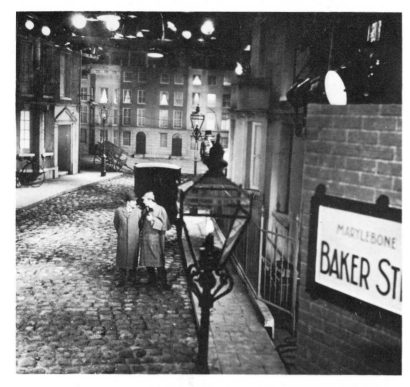

opposite: This extraordinary publicity still of a supposed entrance to 221B (back or front?) emanated from Universal in the 1940s

The Baker Street set built in the studio at Epinay, near Paris, for the Guild Films series of 1954. Howard Marion Crawford and Ronald Howard

Peter Cushing outside the exterior used for Baker Street in the 1968 BBC Television series

133

Home again to the most
remarkable Baker Street set ever,
in *The Private Life of Sherlock
Holmes* (Mirisch 1970). Robert
Stephens, Colin Blakely and Irene
Handl

'The Baker Street set was
unbelievable,' said Robert
Stephens. It was on the whole
back lot at Pinewood, and we did
hardly anything at all on it! It
was all designed by Trauner, and
he very cleverly designed it in
perspective, so that the buildings
actually got smaller.'

In the Footsteps of Sherlock Holmes

Unquestionably the strangest bringing to life of Sherlock Holmes, Dr Watson and other characters from the stories took place in 1968 in Switzerland. Starting as an idea among a few members of the Sherlock Holmes Society of London to spend a week-end in Switzerland and to visit the Reichenbach Falls, it grew and grew, and was firmly taken over by the Swiss National Tourist Office, who are as astute as Sherlock Holmes himself when it comes to spotting a potential publicity coup.

And what a coup it was! The Swiss mania for precision and orderliness was reflected in the faultless organisation of the eight day tour they prepared, but never in their wildest dreams could they have foreseen the triumphant royal progress into which it developed. Certainly the presence of the President of the Society, Sir Paul Gore-Booth, Permanent Head of the Foreign Office, gave status to the venture, and gave the news media an outside chance of a sensational story, should anything go wrong. But that does not account for the extraordinary eruption of interest in the *whole* tour, and not just the two days absence from official duties which was all that Sir Paul Gore-Booth could manage.

Long before the appointed date a number of members of the Society had agreed to participate, although quite a few seem to have looked on the whole notion of cavorting around Europe in fancy dress as rather infra-dig, and so they did not go. Those of us who went had been requested to equip ourselves with Victorian clothing to appear as characters from the Sherlock Holmes stories. 'To make travel more comfortable', we were told, 'it will not be necessary to wear costumes during the entire trip, but only on specific occasions.'

Later on, when we were fully committed to the event, we were informed that 'As the journey now has so many highlights, all the various resorts are expecting the party to be dressed "à la 1890" . . . costumes will be worn on all ceremonial occasions, including travelling on the air flight from London and travelling in Switzerland.'

So there we were at the Swiss Centre, Leicester Square, at 8.30 on a Saturday morning at the end of April 1968, dressed up in Victorian clothes and nonchalantly pretending we did not feel self-conscious. Once inside, it was not so bad, since there were other people similarly dressed, and slowly we began to study the situation. We were supposed to be enjoying a Continental breakfast but perhaps because of suppressed excitement we only managed coffee.

Either the restaurant over-estimated or a lot more people must have
felt like us, because, after we had departed, scores of croissants
were given away to the bystanders outside the Centre.

The Swiss Centre was buzzing with people. Some, with tape
recorders, were interviewing Gore-Booth (who was there to see the
party off) and the other principal characters of the tour. An
extremely smart man in uniform with a leather pouch across his
back was obviously Peterson, the Commissionaire from the story
The Blue Carbuncle, who brings to Sherlock Holmes the remarkable
blue stone found in the crop of a Christmas goose. This Peterson
was really James Holroyd, an eminent Holmesian scholar whose
attention to detail was to be expected: he actually *had* an imitation
goose hanging from his bag.

One person who struck us as decidedly odd was a large man in a
loud mustard-coloured check suit, with a big black waxed
moustache, pince-nez and a round brown hat, who seemed very
active for such an early hour. We spotted one or two faces that we
recognised, despite heavy Victorian disguises, and then the
moustachioed gent in the mustard suit began ushering everyone
outside to start the journey, thus revealing himself as none other
than Albert Kunz, the General Manager of the Swiss Centre and
our courier for the tour.

In the advance programmes the departure was to be in horse-
drawn carriages. When the final printed programme arrived these
were disclosed as 'horse-drawn Whitbread wagons', but it seemed
that we were only to suffer the wagons so far and then change to
coaches. In fact the wagons were not at all bad, and we began to
enjoy looking down on a slightly amazed London populace that was
only just coming to at that time on a Saturday morning.

On our wagon we sat opposite a man in a fawn suit and bowler
hat, accompanied by a young lady. Next to them was Peterson the
Commissionaire, and a young man in a tweed suit and knee-

stockings, with a tweed hat and a rather anxious expression. He was clutching an old brief case and some copies of *The Times*. I was able to see who he was from the label on his case.

We had not gone far when the man in the fawn suit opened out a copy of that morning's *Times* and began commenting on the front page article that dealt with the Tour. I grinned at the young man in tweeds and he grinned back.

'Have you seen this in today's *Times*?' said Fawn-Suit, turning to Peterson. 'This fellow's writing here about Sherlock Holmes sharing a room with Irene Adler. I must say it seems a strange thing to write . . .'

'Before you go any further,' interjected Peterson, 'I think I ought to introduce you to this gentleman next to me. This is Philip Howard of *The Times*. He wrote the article.'

After our parade through London we transferred to a motor coach in Hyde Park to complete the journey to London Airport. On the coach we began comparing personal props with those carried by other members of the party. The couple next to us were Lady Frances Carfax and the Hon Philip Green, from the story *The Disappearance of Lady Frances Carfax*, impersonated by June and Roger Lancelyn Green, and they had spotted the reading matter I was carrying for the journey. It was a *Strand Magazine* of 1891. They had countless family heirlooms such as card cases and spectacles stowed about their persons, most of which were used during the Tour.

At London Airport we were no sooner inside the building when a grating female American voice demanded 'Where's the movie?' Hall Pycroft, dapper in frock coat and top hat, politely explained what we were supposed to be doing. We were all feeling extremely self-conscious, and waiting at the airport was nerve-wracking. Pycroft lit a cigarette.

'That gentleman,' exclaimed Lady Frances, 'is smoking a cigarette in public!' She would make a fine Lady Bracknell.

Because we were still shy about our appearance at that stage, we stood together in small groups, intensely interested in our own conversations. Our legs began to ache and there were only odd seats vacant. Nobody wanted to go and sit alone. Then at last our flight was called.

'Sherlock Holmes and party are requested to board their aircraft through Gate No 1 for the great adventure in Switzerland,' announced a voice in careful Swiss English, and if we had not been noticed before, all eyes were certainly on us as we moved sheepishly towards the exit. At that moment we had our first intimation of the type of response that lay before us, and of how much the magic of Sherlock Holmes still works, for a number of people stood up and beamed and waved, and a crackle of applause sounded through the departure lounge.

We were travelling on a regular Swissair flight, and after we had taken our seats in the Caravelle we were joined by a number of tight-lipped business men in sober suits who occupied the remaining seats with looks of severe disapproval at such childish antics. Here they were, busily trying to close the trade gap, answering the call to export, and generally working their way towards ulcers in the national interest, and all we could do was dress up in Victorian clothes and make ourselves look ridiculous gadding about Switzerland, frittering away valuable non-sterling currency.

Some of them couldn't even bring themselves to look directly at such nonsense. Whether or not they were embarrassed by our company, they certainly were not allowed to forget us. After the usual welcome aboard broadcast in several languages, the captain added 'And a special welcome aboard to our distinguished party travelling in the footsteps of Sherlock Holmes.' And when lunch was served, on each individual tray was a mousse, surmounted by a disc of chocolate on which was fixed a marzipan curly pipe!

In the absence of Sir Paul Gore-Booth for three-quarters of the tour, Sherlock Holmes was impersonated by Anthony Howlett, with whom I had first become interested in Holmesian studies when we were at school together in Grantham. Tony is the first to admit that over the years he has grown too portly to look like Sherlock Holmes, and in fact had originally planned to travel as Sherlock's corpulent brother Mycroft. But when the need for a substitute Sherlock suddenly arose, Tony was both knowledgeable and available, and found himself pitchforked into the principal part.

It was perhaps the most difficult of all impersonations of Sherlock Holmes, for apart from two or three set pieces there were no scripts, no stage directions and no chance for preparations. Everything had to be improvised, and was performed live before the public, for most of each day, in the presence of television and movie cameras, photographers and reporters. Fortunately there is a strong streak of the Ruritanian in Tony, and his enthusiasm for romantic play-acting carried him through this daunting task.

Behind us in the aircraft an Australian was discussing with Tony arrangements for filming the arrival at Geneva. I felt certain I recognised the voice.

'Oh, that's Bob Danvers-Walker,' said Tony. 'Pathé are making a Pathé Pictorial in colour. His camera men will meet us at Geneva and stay with us for the tour.'

So *that* was the voice. Bob Danvers-Walker, the newsreel commentator one still hears on ITV's programme *All Our Yesterdays*; the voice that has announced countless prizes on television quiz shows; the voice that was now saying to Tony, 'Just look at that bloody rain. We'll never get anything in colour if it doesn't stop soon.'

Luckily we flew through the rain to land at a dry airport, and all the ordinary passengers and the photographers were allowed off first, so that the people in costumes could disembark with full ceremony. The business men were so glad to be given some priority at last that they almost collided with some more unusually attired people who were trying to board the aircraft.

'Weirdly attired' is perhaps a better way of describing the first

A Victorian Sunday morning at Lausanne Cathedral. The author and his wife, followed by Hall Pycroft and Mrs Grant Munro (Philip and Patsy Dalton) and Peterson the Commissionaire (James Holroyd)

person to come aboard. It was that bounder Colonel Sebastian Moran, henchman of Professor Moriarty. He was clad in Norfolk suit and old Etonian stockings, with a white topee and a gaudy MCC tie that most other members had long ago refused to wear. His lapel badge declared 'I'll shoot S. Holmes or bust', on his back was a haversack full of assorted weaponry, and he carried in one hand an alpenstock and in the other a transistor radio that converted into a sub-machine gun. Hardly a true Conan Doyle figure but it was evident that Lord Donegall, whom we were just able to detect beneath all that, was playing his role strictly for laughs. As a Swiss resident it was simpler for him to join the party at Geneva.

With him were their Majesties the King and Queen of Bohemia, in the persons of the writers Michael and Mollie Hardwick, who had travelled ahead to make advance arrangements for the tour. We were all marshalled in order by Albert Kunz, and left the aircraft to the strains of a thumping brass band who appeared to be dressed as Victorian firemen. On the tarmac were many more people in costume, some to join the party, some who were part of Albert Kunz's impeccable organisation and some who had just come to welcome us. There followed a speech by the Director of the Geneva Tourist Office, who dwelt rather heavily on Sherlock Holmes's professed desire to travel quietly and unnoticed through Switzerland (hollow laughter from the Press corps). Tony mounted the gangway and uttered a few impromptu words in reply, and we then waited while the horde of photographers took their pictures, after which we proceeded in a wide arc, for the benefit of the movie cameramen, into the airport coach, which carried us a mere 150 yards to the terminal building. This was quite far enough, for the band had already packed themselves into the coach and were thumping away at 'We All Live in a Yellow Submarine'.

Once at the terminal building we just followed in the wake of Albert Kunz who, walking stick held aloft, carved a pathway straight through crowds, band, customs and entrance hall into the street outside, where we boarded coaches for our hotels. We reflected on how easy a smuggling operation would have been. 'Pointless,' said someone. 'Who wants to smuggle things *into* Switzerland?'

Apart from a welcome rest in the afternoon, we had the opportunity to prepare our costumes for that evening's banquet. We had already been in several conversations, and overheard some others, on the problems of equipping for the tour, and it was interesting to compare the efforts that had been made. Some had evidently spent much money at costumiers, while others had made do very effectively with simple but accurate attire. Mrs Grant Munro and Lady Frances each had several changes of hats and dresses, with which they were able to ring the changes most effectively. Some, chiefly among the Press contingent, had made rather perfunctory attempts to be in costume, mainly by wearing wing-collars, bow-ties and deerstalkers, but at least they had taken the trouble. Several gentlemen had allowed their side-whiskers to grow especially for the occasion. This was in 1968, remember, and was at the expense of a certain amount of chaffing from their business and professional friends beforehand, but it saved them all the trouble and discomfort experienced by others who daily affixed to their faces with spirit gum an assortment of sideboards, dundrearies and moustaches. Albert Kunz twice lost his moustache during the tour, but, typical of him, had a spare each time.

The banquet, in honour of Mr & Mrs Adrian Conan Doyle, was at a neighbouring hotel. As it was raining hard we shared a taxi there with the Lancelyn Greens. Our taxi driver was distinctly curious about us. Were we Americans? Were we actors, then? Evidently only Americans or actors would have spent money on a taxi for as short a distance. He seemed not to have noticed the rain.

Efficient young ladies at the Hotel des Bergues produced from a card index individual tickets to identify our table places, and we took our seats marvelling once more at the smooth organisation. The only blemish was the lack of a place for Lady Frances. 'I know

I disappeared in the story,' she observed, 'but this is carrying authenticity a bit far!' The matter was swiftly rectified, and we were able to devote ourselves to a wonderful meal. The wine flowed in profusion, and by the time we reached the liqueurs we didn't really care whether there were crimes, speeches or anything else.

The printed programme had warned that 'During the dinner, a singular and perplexing crime will occur, and those present will join Swiss radio audiences in solving it.' What we did not know, and only pieced together later, was that during the afternoon, while we extras and hangers-on were resting and idling our time away, the principals had been grappling with one crisis after another. Because of the number attending the banquet, the venue was switched to another room. That affected the setting of the crime, and consequently the script needed alteration. The planned hook-up with Swiss radio was on and off several times, and almost at the last moment the hotel staff threatened to strike over the mass of cables and equipment brought in by an army of television camera crews who suddenly invaded the place with no prior arrangement. Albert Kunz dealt with this last little hiatus by simply turning the television people out.

Oblivious of all this drama behind the scenes, we tried hard to concentrate as the programme unfolded. The Master of Ceremonies announced that all the doors would now be closed as the speeches were to begin. The staff obediently banged all the doors, and immediately all the lights went out. After a few moments total darkness the lights went on again and Irene Adler jumped to her feet crying 'My jewels! My necklace! Stolen!'

At that moment no one within 20 feet of her table would have had the remotest chance of escape, for her words were hardly uttered before the table was completely hidden by scores of photographers.

'Mr Holmes,' she continued above the jostle of cameramen and clicking of shutters, 'my necklace has been stolen. It is priceless. It was a gift from my former friend, the King of Bohemia. Mr Holmes, although we were once adversaries, I implore you to recover my jewels.'

It would have been difficult for Holmes to refuse such a moving request, particularly as Irene Adler on this occasion was portrayed by a very attractive young blonde actress, Dominique Joos, substituting for Lady Gore-Booth who was joining us later with her husband. Sherlock Holmes begged the indulgence of the assembled company for a few moments while he solved this little problem, and proceeded to conduct a swift investigation. We were all issued with forms (English or French, as you wished) on which we were expected to answer several questions, but I don't think our brains were up to it by then. The King of Bohemia attempted to incriminate Professor Moriarty and Colonel Moran, and was considerably discomfited when Sherlock Holmes demonstrated that the King himself had stolen the necklace.

There were speeches by various exalted personages, and one by

Adrian Conan Doyle welcomes Sherlock Holmes to the Château de Lucens. (Albert Kunz, in check suit, has not had time to replace his fugitive moustache)

Adrian Conan Doyle and his usual line of father-boosting. What a pity he never realised that Sir Arthur Conan Doyle was too big a man to need anyone rushing to his defence every five minutes.

When it was all over some of us relaxed together in one of the hotel bars, still only gradually becoming accustomed to our new Victorian personalities. 'It's all so unreal!' said Lady Frances. 'So *real*, you mean,' corrected Peterson. 'We shall be going back to unreality next week!'

The next morning was bright and sunny and we went down to breakfast already dressed in our costumes. The few men in the dining room eyed us with sympathetic interest but we were immersed in *La Suisse Dimanche*, which had lavished a whole page on our arrival. Their roving reporter 'Rouletabille' was accompanying the tour and evidently intended to devote a daily column to our activities. I wondered if his choice of pseudonym was accidental, for Rouletabille was the detective in the lurid crime novels of Gaston Leroux.

After breakfast motor coaches conveyed us to the lakeside at Versoix, where we waited in the glorious sunshine. A surfeit of photographers caused the landing stage to tilt alarmingly, and we had to move to safety. Martin Rolfe, the Pathé cameraman, passed the time taking interesting shots of the King and Queen of Bohemia nodding condescendingly to the peasants.

A hydrofoil took us across the lake to Lausanne, where an astonishing crowd had gathered. This time the band was bigger and much better. The Mayor made a charming speech of welcome, referring warmly to the affection everyone has for Sherlock Holmes. Tony replied, with suitable arm-wavings, and justice having been done we boarded an ancient and curious chain-driven beer lorry and began climbing the steep hills of Lausanne, preceded by a flashy police motor-cycle escort. The lorry was immaculate but terrifying; every time it changed gear we were in danger of rolling back downhill during the dreadful pauses. That would have made rather a mess of the procession of cars behind us which included several with cameramen riding on the wings, trying to outdo one another with exclusive shots, and one car whose driver was operating a camera with one hand and the steering wheel with the other.

Our destination was Lausanne Cathedral, where a short service had been arranged for us. The Reverend Ian MacCullough preached on one of Holmes's own axioms – 'When you have eliminated the impossible, whatever remains, however improbable, must be the truth' – which he related to the recent festival of Easter.

By the time we reached the Chalet Suisse for lunch, we were sweltering in the heat. Tony removed his overcoat and cape and posed for the photographers on one of the police motor-cycles. Once inside we followed his example and removed our frock coats. The gentlemen with fancy waistcoats had a definite touch of the Mississippi riverboat gambler about them, and the lunch party had that sort of gaiety too. Whatever ice remained to be broken went during lunch that day, and we were in a joyous mood when the coaches took us to the Château de Lucens that afternoon. In the courtyard we were met by Adrian Conan Doyle in person, who said a few words of welcome to Tony, the ostensible leader of the party, who replied. This was then repeated twice, since neither Pathé nor the television cameramen had got the shots they wanted.

A *Vin d'honneur* was served in the courtyard, while we watched Swiss dancers and heard Swiss singers, all performing especially for us. After the hilarious luncheon we had enjoyed perhaps we were unwise to sample so many of the Swiss wines pressed on us, but it was so hot and we were thirsty . . . When at last the time came to see the displays which formed the Conan Doyle Foundation, then established by Adrian at Lucens, we were glad to drag ourselves inside out of the sun. The galleries of Conan Doyle material were disappointingly small, but the reproduction of the Baker Street room revived our flagging spirits. It was the 1951 Exhibition room improved and expanded beyond our highest hopes, and when we arrived in it Pathé were busy filming Sherlock Holmes and Doctor Watson, seated beside the fireplace. 'No flash while we're shooting, boys,' Bob Danvers-Walker entreated the photographers, '*please, no flash.*' He was dodging about inside the room directing the proceedings in spite of our unhelpful attempts to distract Tony, and to make him laugh while he pretended to play the violin, a performance that had us in stitches instead.

The Dr Watson with Tony was Dr Maurice Campbell, who was then the only surviving member of the original pre-war Sherlock Holmes Society. Maurice was an eminent physician and an erudite Holmesian scholar, and although then 78 he took his full part in the rigorous activities of the tour.

Dr Maurice Campbell and Tony
Howlett in the Baker Street room

As usual none of the camera crews had been able to agree to film
simultaneously, and Holmes and Watson had been in and out of the
replica room several times. It was the final straw when the German
television team insisted on filming and recording live.

'But what are we to say?' protested Tony.

'Oh, that doesn't matter. Just make up some typical Holmesian
dialogue,' came the airy reply.

'Very well,' said Tony, grimly, but there was a twinkle in Maurice
Campbell's eye.

They returned to their seats by the fire and when the camera was
rolling, Maurice leaned towards Tony and gestured at a newspaper
he was holding.

'I say, Holmes,' he began, 'have you seen this Police Gazette.
These German television people come in here and mess everybody
about and want us to perform dialogue with no preparation. I think
it's absolutely disgraceful!'

He slapped down the newspaper. 'There! Let them use *that*
soundtrack if they can.'

Outside in one of the corridors we bumped into Adrian.

'Have you been to the armoury yet,' he enquired, 'and the
Nuremberg Maiden? You *must* see those.'

'Just on our way,' we said, and we meant to, but we were
exhausted, and sneaked off to the motor coach and back to our
hotel instead.

As nothing was planned for that evening we had time to re-cuperate before the next very full day, which began at Lausanne University, where we and many of the students gathered to hear a lecture by Professor J. Mathyer, Director of the Institute of Criminology at the University, on 'Modern Scientific Methods in Criminal Investigation'. The lecture was in French (we had a simultaneous translation on headphones), and was a very long and serious discourse, to which I gave a polite vote of thanks.

Up to that point the students all listened with great attention; then the fun began. Dr Watson proposed, and Hall Pycroft (Philip Dalton) seconded the motion for debate, 'That Sherlock Holmes is the greatest detective of all time', which was naturally opposed by Professor Moriarty (Charles Scholefield, QC) and Colonel Moran.

It seems that Professor Mathyer and the students had gained the impression that we were representatives of a learned criminological association, and that when the debate began they were in for some really deep stuff. Their surprise at our appearance all in costume was nothing to their bewilderment as the debate got under way, with all the usual tongue-in-cheek humour and scholarly side-swiping that our tame Holmesian experts indulge in so skilfully and, to the outsider, so seriously.

The students' note-taking gradually ceased and a look of incredu-lous dismay appeared on their faces. It was not so much a failure in organisation at the University as a flaw in the imagination. Their perplexity plainly deepened as the motion was voted upon and carried, it seemed to me, more as an act of faith than as the result of persuasive debating.

The *coup de grace* came when the King of Bohemia (Michael Hardwick), resplendent in his red and blue Ivor Novello uniform, stepped on to the platform and addressed us as if we were the Bohemian populace. He announced the winners of the crime prob-lem at the banquet, and then, because of the affront to his royal person in being accused of that crime, declared that henceforth all bars in Bohemia would be closed between 4 and 5 am.

'Will you all please stand,' he said, as straight-faced as ever, and we all obeyed.

'My little people, if you know the Bohemian National Anthem you can sing it,' he concluded, and walked off the platform.

We determined amongst ourselves that he would jolly well have a Bohemian National Anthem before much longer. As we dispersed from the auditorium the students eyed us with distrust. 'You're all fakes! ' said one.

In the afternoon we enjoyed a beautiful train journey up the Rhône Valley to Sion, where yet again enormous crowds awaited us. A large fife-and-drum band in Cantonal costume led us in procession through all the principal streets, which were lined with schoolchildren all holding Union Jacks and Swiss flags. We had soon relaxed into our respective roles, and had time to study the public's reactions while we waved and doffed our hats.

The small children were all delighted at the spectacle, while the

older children, sophisticated 12-year-olds and the like, were rather puzzled. The old people relished the pageant, especially the grannies who were clearly thrilled to see some of their memories come to life, and who occasionally popped back indoors and dragged out a younger relative to illustrate to them what they had often spoken about. Many of the young and middle-aged adults were uncertain what their response ought to be, and in a few cases were obviously embarrassed. By that time we felt no embarrassment whatsoever. After all, we were the ones who were perfectly normal and real.

That evening we gathered in the deep wine-cellar of an ancient chateau for a wine-tasting contest, in which we were set questions with clear allusions to the Sherlock Holmes stories, but which was really an excuse for promoting Swiss wines. The small cellar was packed with people and with camera crews, who at one point were almost filming each other's exposure meters, and there was a mixed aroma of melting Swiss cheese and scorching electric cables hung too close to someone else's lights. Albert Kunz, in inviting the news media for the tour, had from the outset laid great emphasis on wearing Victorian apparel if at all possible. The Germans had treated the request in a typically thorough and literal fashion, and we sat in the cellar watching cameramen and technicians perspiring in frock coats and false moustaches as they humped around cameras, lights and heavy equipment. What with them and the official entertainment, the food, wine and company, it was another amazing evening.

Over a few brandies, back at our hotel, we resumed our plans for a National Anthem, and I undertook to write the words. At breakfast next morning we wanted Albert Kunz's assistance, but he was busy with other matters. He had already been on the phone to London and could tell us how many minutes and seconds coverage the tour had been given in the previous evening's radio and tele-

vision news bulletins, and what that morning's newspapers said. It
was, he confided to one of his colleagues, 'un succès énorme.'

Unfortunately Albert was losing his voice, which was hardly
surprising with all the talking and directing he had to do. We had
to be shepherded everywhere, and with a success of such unexpected
magnitude on his hands, he was not neglecting *any* personal attention to ensure a safe climax and completion. So when, on the train
to Kandersteg, he came through asking for 'two horse ladies,' mean-
ing two ladies to ride on horseback, our amusement puzzled him.
So did the disappearance of a number of us into the observation
car for most of the journey. We were rehearsing.

At Kandersteg we really began to get into the story of *The Final
Problem*, in which Moriarty is following Holmes and Watson across
Switzerland, and Watson relates that 'a large rock clattered down
and roared into the lake behind us'. Sure enough, when we arrived
in the town centre, in a variety of ancient transport, there was a
huge rock, apparently all of 3 or 4 tons, which Sherlock Holmes
duly inspected with his magnifying glass, whereupon it was carted
away shoulder high by four ancient mountain guides. Although it
was only mid-morning Kandersteg was not going to be outdone in
hospitality, and we were given 'elevenses' of wine and cheese-cakes
before reboarding the train. At last we cornered Albert Kunz and
asked him to delay their Majesties until we had all disembarked at
Interlaken. He did so, without asking why, and when they finally
emerged into the station yard Peterson conducted us in three verses
of doggerel to the tune of the old 100th.

The King was so pleased that he decreed all the bars should be
re-opened, and Albert Kunz was so tickled at this spontaneous piece
of party fun that after we had ridden in open carriages to Neuhaus,
he insisted on having the Anthem performed again. The King ordered
me to kneel and proceeded to knight me with my own walking-stick.

HM the King knights the author
of the Anthem

The whole business had been hard enough for the foreign Press men to grasp when we started, but now they were getting right out of their depth. A Dutch journalist regarded the Anthem as of great significance, and copied all the words from my notebook into his in all seriousness. Albert Kunz wanted a copy to have it duplicated. I tried to explain that we intended to alter the words as we went along, but it was no use; before lunch was over his staff were distributing copies wholesale.

On the putting green at Neuhaus we witnessed the arrival of Sir Paul and Lady Gore-Booth to take over their roles. Sir Paul and Tony approached each other. 'You impostor!' they cried.

The handing-over was simple. Tony merely doffed his deerstalker and donned a round black hat. 'Instant Mycroft,' he explained.

An ancient paddle-steamer was brought back to convey us along the lake from Interlaken to Brienz, where an equally ancient train of railway carriages of 1888 took us to the principal place of the tour – the tiny town of Meiringen, nearest point to the Reichenbach Falls.

We thought we had seen huge crowds, but Meiringen was like Wembley on Cup Final day. In *The Final Problem* Conan Doyle had Holmes and Watson staying at an hotel which he called the Englischer Hof, so one of the hotels had its signs obliterated and for 48 hours was re-named the Englischer Hof (no half-measures for the Swiss), and it was there that we all processed, as our horse-drawn carriages forced their way through the unbelievable mass of people.

On the steps of the hotel came Albert Kunz's big moment. Representing Peter Steiler, the proprietor who cared for Holmes and Watson, he made a little speech of welcome to his hotel that we had been hearing him rehearse on several train journeys.

Inside, the deputy mayor bade us welcome on behalf of the town, and Gore-Booth, with diplomacy and aplomb befitting the head of the Foreign Office, replied in faultless German, a touch which

'You impostor!' Tony Howlett relinquishes the role of Sherlock Holmes to Sir Paul Gore-Booth

delighted the citizens. What delighted *us* was the Director of Tourism for Meiringen announcing the programme for the following day, when he alluded to Sir Paul *Bore-Gooth* and Lady Irene Adler.

Wednesday was the great day, when the final encounter between Sherlock Holmes and Professor Moriarty was to be re-enacted at 2.30 p.m., but so that the news media could get their film and photos in time for the evening television bulletins and newspapers, the death struggle was specially staged for the Press in the morning as well, and we were free until lunchtime. A walk through the town made it clear that this was the biggest event ever to have happened in Meiringen, and all the shops and businesses had been enlisted in publicising the occasion. Every shop window had a Sherlock Holmes poster, the bakers had cakes with the Holmesian silhouette on, confectioners had Sherlock Holmes marzipan chocolates, everyone had something appropriate on display, and across the main street

Notice to the citizens of Meiringen
to support the great occasion

was a huge banner welcoming Sherlock Holmes to Meiringen.

Trade must have prospered, for there were in the town that day 127 representatives of the world's news media, including two from the Tass news agency and a reporter from Pakistan. ITN flew in by helicopter for the day, whereas the BBC were with us for five out of the eight days. Italian and Swiss television newsmen were around most of the time, and other reporters and crews came and went at various stages of the tour. Once the newsmen had realised that we really *were* just having a little gentle fun in which they were welcome to join, they entered into the party spirit and gave us almost as much entertainment as the official arrangements. 'It is impossible to send up this expedition,' wrote Barry Norman in *The Daily Mail*. 'It has been quietly sending itself up from the start.' Well, *he* went off on another assignment and a day or so later I saw him on a station platform as our train pulled in. 'Can't you tear yourself away?' I enquired. 'No. I must see how it all ends,' he admitted.

At lunch, which was held half way up the mountain, we found the principals in a state of exhaustion, having performed the death-struggle six times! Not only could the various crews not agree to co-operate in filming together, but Pathé refused to change Holmeses in mid-film, understandably, and Tony had to repeat what had already been done.

Death struggle at the Reichenbach Falls

We walked down to the observation platform beside the falls, and

150

the sight did not disappoint us. Conan Doyle's description, 'that dreadful cauldron of swirling water and seething foam', had often seemed a rather purple passage, but he had in no way exaggerated. We looked across the chasm at the inexorable progress of the final encounter, all exactly as in *The Final Problem*. Holmes and Watson strolled along the ledge and chatted for some time. Below, on another path Moriarty despatched a messenger to decoy Watson back to the hotel. Watson was duly lured away, and Moriarty ascended to the ledge and confronted Holmes. They talked, they struggled, disappeared momentarily from view and then two bodies went over the edge and hurtled down to their certain doom. It could not possibly have been done better, and we applauded the faithful rendering of that well-known episode. The two dummies were later hauled up on the cords with which they had been recovered several times in the morning.

The funicular railway went out of order and we descended to the bottom of the falls by walking down the track. When all were eventually assembled, the Mayor lamented the recent tragic episode in which were lost a great professor of mathematics, although criminally disposed, and the greatest criminal investigator. It was a sad day indeed. 'Do not grieve,' said Gore-Booth, suddenly emerging from a shrubbery and making another charming little speech in German, explaining that it was only Moriarty who had gone over, and he, Sherlock Holmes, was alive and well, and he unveiled a plaque to himself to prove it, whereupon the band began playing the current popular song *Puppet on a String*. (Who says the Swiss have no sense of humour?) Then the plaque was covered up and Tony did it all again, just for Pathé!

The Mayor said that obviously it was an occasion for rejoicing, and a grand Swiss country evening would be held to celebrate. Henceforth 1st May in Meiringen will be Sherlock Holmes Day, and a public holiday. Since 1st May is Labour Day and already a public holiday, there should be no problems there.

The Swiss country evening was another colossal party, with Swiss singing, dancing, yodelling and Alpine horn blowing, as well as the customary speech of HM the King, the Bohemian National Anthem and the other family jokes that had become a regular part of the proceedings.

Next morning all the schoolchildren from Meiringen and miles around were gathered at the station to see us off. We had to sign countless autographs before we could get on the train, and they serenaded us with little songs in English, Italian and German as the train drew out.

When the train reached Lucerne it was Tony who stepped off as Sherlock Holmes. On the station platform we were stopped in our tracks by the *British* National Anthem played over the loudspeaker system. (The King of Bohemia was purple.) A cavalcade of veteran cars, taxis and buses took us off to the Lucerne Transport Museum, and watching us leave the station stood two people who resembled an English diplomat and his wife, looking conventional, and wistful.

Our guide at the Transport Museum was quite incapable of deviating from the would-be comic patter he habitually used. He made disparaging remarks about the quaintness of some of the exhibits, and pointed out, on enlargements of old photographs, the highly amusing old-fashioned passengers, ladies in funny hats, men with big moustaches, and so on. We could scarcely believe our ears, but managed to get rid of him when we came to a balloon basket, suspended from the ceiling. The photographers wanted someone in the basket, but our guide demurred, and said he would have to ask Herr So-and-so. As soon as he had disappeared we bundled two of the ladies in the basket, the photos were taken, and we went out, glad to be free of his facetious comments.

We sat in the sunshine on the deck of a steamer exhibit in the museum grounds, dawdling over coffee. 'I have to keep pinching myself,' said Lady Frances, slightly breathless after her brief balloon trip. 'Is all this really happening?' We assured her it was.

'When I am back home at the sink,' she declared, 'I shall close my eyes and say "I believe in Sherlock Holmes and Dr Watson, the Royal Family of Bohemia, the Neville St Clairs . . . " '

At Gütsch it was Professor Moriarty's turn to pay a graceful tribute to Queen Victoria, who had stayed there exactly 100 years previously. The usual sumptuous luncheon was enlivened by more Swiss entertainment, followed by a performer who was given a tremendous build-up, Kim Hong Chul, the world's only Korean Swiss yodeller, self-taught in Korea from Swiss recordings. He was indescribably bad. BBC reporter John Bierman, who took two days leave to finish the tour when the BBC team went home, recorded an interview with the Korean. It was so bizarre that nobody back at the BBC would believe it was anything but a hoax.

Three consecutive train journeys took us eastwards across Switzerland, ending at Davos late in the evening, and as our train pulled in, a smart Swiss Army band was playing for us. In an impromptu move, Sherlock Holmes, HM the King and Peterson the Commissionaire gave the band a thorough inspection. Weary after a gruelling journey, we enjoyed the luxury apartments reserved for us, and particularly the champagne in the refrigerators.

The purpose of the visit to Davos was to pay homage to the creator of Sherlock Holmes, Sir Arthur Conan Doyle, and next morning we assembled in the municipal park to see a plaque to Sir Arthur unveiled by Sherlock Holmes and Adrian Conan Doyle. The Swiss have good reason to be fond of Sir Arthur, for he was a pioneer of winter sports in Switzerland, introducing skiing, and Adrian had with him the skis on which his father performed the first crossing on skis of the Maienfelder Furka Pass, between Davos and Arosa, in March, 1894. In the town hall Michael Hardwick, shedding his role of HM the King, delivered a generous tribute to Sir Arthur, but for whose literary skill none of us would have been there.

The cable car station, normally closed out of season, was opened especially for us and we ascended to the summit of the Jakobshorn,

We hereby publish
and declare
that the title of

HONORARY CITIZEN

has been conferred upon

SHERLOCK HOLMES

with all extraordinary privileges
by the community of

MEIRINGEN
REICHENBACH-FALLS

and that this day the first of May
nineteen hundred sixty eight
is proclaimed
Meiringen's Sherlock Holmes Day

The President   The Secretary

where the restaurant was also opened for us, and after lunch Pathé carried out some more filming of Holmes, Watson and the villains. We descended again to Davos, thus relieving headaches brought on by the altitude, the ear-splitting orchestra at lunch, and tiredness. There in the station yard was the Army band again, playing away. They had been so impressed at being inspected by such important persons the night before that they had asked if they could return to play us off, and, as they were being inspected a second time, into the station steamed our own Victorian 'special' – an ancient steam locomotive, with top-hatted driver, pulling four Victorian carriages – and away we puffed to Chur, stopping on the way to let the photographers and cameramen get off and take all they wanted. At Chur we had to transfer to the mountain railway line to climb the

154

steep valley to Arosa, where we dined informally in non-Victorian garb, and nobody recognised anybody.

The next morning it was up another mountain, the Hörnli, and lunch looking down on countless mountain tops. A special demonstration using old skis and ski sticks was given, and a display by young ski champions. Then down in the gondola cars to Arosa, on down to Chur and the long train ride to Zurich.

The champion brass band of all Switzerland, 100 strong, was at the station, waiting to march us right through the centre of Zürich,

Rathbone on record; in Caedmon's *Silver Blaze . . .*

where everything was brought to a standstill by us and the immense crowds. Our destination was the Carlton Pub, which the Swiss fondly imagine to be typically English. There a 'mysterious drink of the month' was served in glasses decorated with a message in the alphabet from *The Dancing Men* story. One visitor asked my wife to decipher it for him, and said, 'Well, you should know what it says. You're an actress, aren't you?' He must have seen the *Luzerner Tageblatt,* which had described us as the Sherlock Holmes touring company.

Sherlock Holmes asked us all to return our glasses to the bar, to be washed and given to us later, and then to follow him. Out we all went through a side street into the gigantic Union Bank of Switzerland, where some more skulduggery was attempted, involving Victorian Swiss policemen, a Swiss bank director in a fancy waistcoat and a bar of gold, impersonated by real policemen, a real bank director and a real bar of gold. Sherlock Holmes solved it all rapidly, and Dr Kampfen, head of the Swiss Tourist Office, then thanked everyone for taking part in the tour. By the time the regular string of speeches, royal decrees, National Anthems, etc, had been gone through the whole band had moved into the main hall of the bank, and began to play popular tunes. All the young ladies of the bank were stationed at their counters, issuing us with souvenirs: the Dancing Men glasses, little bags of gold coins (with chocolate centres) from 'The Gnomes of Zürich', and beautiful diplomas certifying that we had undertaken this amazing pilgrimage.

Young girls in Swiss national costume were serving yet more Swiss wines, the photographers began dancing with the bank girls, everyone else joined in, and John Bierman was heart-broken that the BBC camera team was not present to capture those final crazy moments. 'If only we'd known *this* was going to happen . . .' he lamented.

Well, how could we have known? If someone had said that at 10 o'clock on a Saturday evening we should be inside the biggest bank in Zürich, in Victorian costume, drinking and dancing to a brass band, who would have believed it?

Three great voices: Gielgud as Holmes, Richardson as Watson, and Orson Welles as Moriarty, on Decca

156

THE ORIGINAL CAST ALBUM OF BAKER STREET

MGM's recording on the 1965 musical with original cast

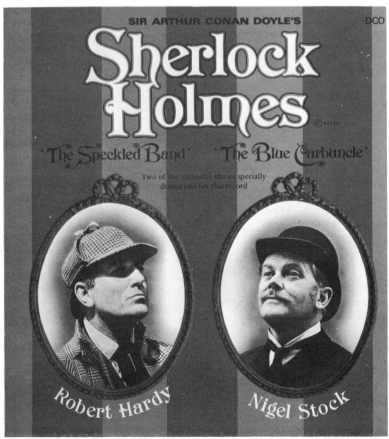

Robert Hardy never appeared like this as Holmes; his performances were confined to a series of plays specially written for records by Michael and Mollie Hardwick. They produced eight superb sound dramas, in which Hardy gave an excellent demonstration of how well Sherlock Holmes can be played

Appendix

A check list of appearances of Sherlock Holmes (H) and Dr. Watson (W) in the various entertainment media. Fuller details of most of the productions will be found in *The Public Life of Sherlock Holmes* by Michael Pointer (David & Charles 1975).

STAGE PRODUCTIONS
1. *Under the Clock* 1893. Charles Brookfield (H), Seymour Hicks (W).
2. *Sherlock Holmes* (by Charles Rogers) 1894. John Webb (H), St. John Hamund (W). In South Africa, 1902: Roy Redgrave (H), Reginald Wykeham (W).
3. *Bransby Williams* (H) 1898. Character sketches on the music halls.
4. *Sherlock Holmes* (by William Gillette) 1899. In USA, William Gillette (H), Bruce McRae (W). In London 1901, Gillette (H) and Percy Lyndal (W). Also in USA as Holmes: Herbert Kelcey, Robert Warwick, John Wood, Patrick Horgan, John Neville, Robert Stephens. In GB as Holmes: H. A. Saintsbury, Julian Royce, Kenneth Rivington, T. A. Shannon, Henry S. Dacre, J. S. Crawley, Fred Sargent, Ernest Bliss, George Henry, H. Lawrence Leyton, Henry Renouf, H. Hamilton Stewart, Harold Holland, Laurence Carter, Leonard Tremayne, Leo Trood, Hamilton Deane, John Blake, Noel Howlett, Alfred Burke, John Wood. In Denmark as Holmes: Dorph-Petersen, Vilhelm Birch, Otto Lagoni, Albrecht Schmidt, Herman Florents. In Holland as Holmes: Marcel Myin, Eduard Verkade. In Sweden as Holmes: Hr. Bergendorff, Hr. Bergvall, Knut Nyblom, Emil Ljungqvist, Hugo Ronnblad, William Larsson. In Australia: Cuyler Hastings (H), F. Lumsden Hare (W). In Germany: Franz Scharwenka (H).
5. *The Bank of England* GB 1900. John F. Preston (H). In USA, 1904, Eugene Moore (H). Also in GB (as H) ST John Beecher, Hubert S. Chambers, Charles H. Lester.
6. *Sherlock Holmes, Detective* or *The Sign of the Four* USA 1901. Richard Butler (H), Carl Smith Seerle (W).
7. *Sheerluck Jones* or *Why D'Gillette Him Off?* GB 1901. A burlesque on Gillette's play. Clarence Blakiston (Jones).
8. *An Adventure in the Life of Sherlock Holmes* GB 1902. John Lawson (H). Also W. R. Perceval (H).
9. *The Great Detective* GB 1902. Roy Redgrave (H).
10. *Sherlock Holmes* (by H. Leslie Bell) GB 1902.
11. *Surelock Holmes* USA 1902. Walter R. Seymour (H).
12. *Sherlock Holmes* (by William Felton) GB 1902. William Felton (H).
13. *Charles Conway* GB 1902. Quick-change artiste in character sketch as Holmes.
14. *The Sign of the Four* USA 1903. Walter Edwards (H), Joseph Rawley (W).
15. *The Painful Predicament of Sherlock Holmes* USA 1905. William Gillette (H).
16. *Sherlock Holmes* (by Fr. von Schontau) Germany 1905.

17. *The Burglar and the Lady* USA 1906. Arthur V. Johnson (H).
18. *The Heart of London* GB 1906 (?). C. York (H), J. Hart (W).
19. *Sherlock Holmes* (by Ferdinand Bonn) Germany 1906. Ferdinand Bonn (H).
20. *Der Hund von Baskerville* Germany 1907. Ferdinand Bonn (H). In Denmark: Emil Wulff (H).
21. *A Night with the Stars* GB 1907. Carl Lynn (H).
22. *Sherlock Holmes* (by L. Ottomeyer) Germany 1907.
23. *Sherlock Holmes* (by P. Rahnheld) Germany 1907.
24. *Sherlock Holmes in Gebirge* Germany 1907.
25. *Sherlock Holmes* (by Pierre Decourcelle) France 1907. Firmin Gémier (H), Saillard (W). Also, Harry Baur (H).
26. *Holmes y Rafles* Spain 1908.
27. *La Garra de Holmes* Spain 1908.
28. *Sherlock Holmes* (by K. Weiss) Germany 1908.
29. *La Captura de Raffles* Spain 1908. Sr. Olivar (H), Sr. Salom (W).
30. *Nadie Mas Fuerte que Sherlock Holmes* Spain 1909. Sr. Guixer (H).
31. *A Study in Scarlet* Denmark 1909. Carl Alstrup (H).
32. *The Speckled Band* GB 1910. H. A. Saintsbury (H), Claude King (W). In USA, Charles Millward (H), Ivo Dawson (W). Also in GB as Holmes: Julian Royce, O. P. Heggie, Grendon Bentley, E. Vassal Vaughan, A. Corney Grain, Herbert Bradford, Sydney Bland, Charles York, R. Goodyer-Kettley, Herbert Stanton, H. A. Young, Harold V. Neilson, Henry Oscar, Robert Gilbert, Rupert Lister, Alan Moore, Donald Gee. Also in Sweden: Einar Froberg (H); in USA: H. Cooper-Cliffe (H); in France: Edward Stirling.
33. *La Aguja Hueca* Spain 1912.
34. *The Raffle-ing of Sherlock Holmes* GB 1913.
35. *La Tragedia de Baskerville* Spain 1915. Sr. Comes (H), Sr. Socias (W).
36. *El Vendedor de Cadaveres* Mallorca 1915.
37. *Hazanas de Sherlock Holmes* Spain 1915. Sr. Parreno (H).
38. *The Crown Diamond* GB 1921. Dennis Neilson-Terry (H), R. V. Taylour (W).
39. *The Return of Sherlock Holmes* GB 1923. Eille Norwood (H), H. G. Stoker (W). Also in GB as Holmes: Charles Buckmaster, Tod Slaughter, Geoffrey Edwards. In Holland: Henry de Vries (H); in Denmark: Herman Florents (H).
40. *The Devil's Servant* GB c 1927 (?).
41. *The Houseboat on the Styx* USA 1928.
42. *The Holmeses of Baker Street* GB 1933. Felix Aylmer (H), Sir Nigel Playfair (W). Also in GB: Edmund Kennedy (H), E. Wensley Russell (W). In USA, 1936: Cyril Scott (H), Conway Wingfield (W).
43. *The Great Detective* (Ballet) GB 1953. Kenneth Macmillan (The Great Detective), Stanley Holden (his friend the Doctor).
44. *Sherlock Holmes* (by Ouida Rathbone) USA 1953. Basil Rathbone (H), Jack Raine (W).
45. *They Might Be Giants* GB 1961. Harry H. Corbett (Justin Playfair, the Holmes character), Avis Bunnage (W).
46. *Baker Street* USA 1961. Fritz Weaver (H), Peter Sallis (W).
47. *Sherlock Holmes and the Speckled Band* GB 1968. Roger Heathcott (H), Clive Rust (W).
48. *The Hound of the Baskervilles* GB 1971. Tim Preece (H), Richard Simpson (W).
49. *Sherlock Holmes and the Affair of the Amorous Regent* USA 1972. Charters H. Anderson (H), John McKay (W).
50. *Sherlock's Last Case* GB 1974. Julian Glover (H), Peter Bayliss

(W). Also in GB: Clyde Pollitt (H), Martin Matthews (W);
Nicholas le Prevost (H), Nick Stringer (W).

51. *Sherlock Holmes of Baker Street* GB 1974. Richard Franklin (H),
Lionel Thomson (W). Also in GB: Brandon Brady (H), Patrick
Mouleton (W).

52. *The Hound of the Baskervilles* USA 1975. Roger Hatch (H), Frank
Dwyer (W).

53. *Sherlock Holmes in Scandal in Bohemia* USA 1975. John Wylie
(H), William Pitts (W).

54. *Sherlock Holmes* (by William Oakley, based on Gillette) USA 1976.
Bryan Foster (H), Terry Rhoades (W).

SILENT FILMS

1. *Sherlock Holmes Baffled* USA 1900.
2. *The Adventures of Sherlock Holmes* USA 1905. Maurice Costello (H).
3. *Sherlock Holmes Returns* ? 1906–7.
4. *Rival Sherlock Holmes* Italy 1907.
5. *Sherlock Hochmes* Hungary 1908. Bauman Karoly (H).
6. *Sherlock Holmes I Livsfare* Denmark 1908. Viggo Larsen (H).
7. *Sherlock Holmes II* Denmark 1908. Viggo Larsen (H).
8. *Sherlock Holmes III* Denmark 1908. Viggo Larsen (H).
9. *Sherlock Holmes in the Great Murder Mystery* USA 1908.
10. *Sangarindens Diamanter* Denmark 1909. Viggo Larsen (H).
11. *Droske No 519* Denmark 1909. Viggo Larsen (H).
12. *Den Graa Dame* Denmark 1909. Viggo Larsen (H).
13. *The Latest Triumph of Sherlock Holmes* France 1909.
14. *Sherlock Holmes* Italy 1910.
15. *Der Alte Sekretär* Germany 1910. Viggo Larsen (H).
16. *Der Blaue Diamant* Germany 1910. Viggo Larsen (H).
17. *Die Falschen Rembrandts* Germany 1910. Viggo Larsen (H).
18. *Sherlock Holmes I Bondefangerklør* Denmark 1910. Otto Lagoni (H).
19. *Die Flucht* Germany 1910. Viggo Larsen (H).
20. *Forklaedte Barnepige* Denmark 1910.
21. *Medlem af den Sorte Hand* Denmark 1910. Holger Rasmussen (H).
22. *Millionobligation* Denmark 1910. Alwin Neuss (H).
23. *Hotel Mysterierne* Denmark 1911.
24. *Arsène Lupins Ende* Germany 1911. Viggo Larsen (H).
25. *Sherlock Holmes contra Professor Moryarty* Germany 1911. Viggo
Larsen (H).
26. *Les Aventures de Sherlock Holmes* France 1911. Henri Gouget (H).
27. *Schlau, Schlauer, am Schlauesten* France 1911.
28—35 were all made in GB in 1912, with Georges Treville (H).
*The Speckled Band, The Reygate Squires, The Beryl Coronet,
The Adventure of the Copper Beeches, A Mystery of Boscombe
Vale, The Stolen Papers, Silver Blaze, The Musgrave Ritual.*
36. *Sherlock Holmes Solves the Sign of the Four* USA 1913. Harry
Benham (H).
37. *Griffard's Claw* Italy 1913.
38. *Sherlock Holmes contra Dr. Mors* Germany 1914 (?). Ferdinand
Bonn (H).
39. *Der Hund von Baskerville* Germany 1914. Alwin Neuss (H).
40. *En Raedsom Nat* Denmark 1914.
41. *Das Einsame Haus* Germany 1914. Alwin Neuss (H).
42. *Hvem er Hun?* Denmark 1914.
43. *A Study in Scarlet* GB 1914. James Bragington (H).
44. *A Study in Scarlet* USA 1914. Francis Ford (H).
45. *Das Unheimliche Zimmer* Germany 1915. Alwin Neuss (H).
46. *Wie Entstand der Hund von Baskerville* Germany 1915. Alwin
Neuss (H).

47. *Das Dunkle Schloss* Germany 1915. Eugen Burg (H).
48. *Ein Schrei in der Nacht* Germany 1915. Alwin Neuss (H).
49. *William Voss* Germany 1915.
50. *Sherlock Holmes* USA 1916. William Gillette (H), Edward Fielding (W).
51. *The Valley of Fear* GB 1916. H. A. Saintsbury (H), Arthur M. Cullin (W).
52. *Sherlock Holmes auf Urlaub* Germany 1916.
53. *Sherlock Holmes Nächtliche Begegnung* Germany 1917.
54. *Der Erdstrommotor* Germany 1917. Hugo Flink (H).
55. *Die Kasette* Germany 1917. Hugo Flink (H).
56. *Der Schlangenring* Germany 1917. Hugo Flink (H).
57. *Die Indische Spinne* Germany 1918. Hugo Flink (H).
58. *Rotterdam-Amsterdam* Germany 1918. Viggo Larsen (H).
59. *Was er im Spiegel sah* Germany 1918. Ferdinand Bonn (H). l).
60. *Die Giftplombe* Germany 1918. Ferdinand Bonn (H).
61. *Das Schicksal der Renate Yongk* Germany 1918. Ferdinand Bonn (H).
62. *Die Dose des Kardinals* Germany 1918. Ferdinand Bonn (H).
63. *Drei Tage Tot* Germany 1919.
64. *Der Mord im Splendid Hotel* Germany 1919. Kurt Brenkendorff (H).
65. *Dr. Macdonalds Sanatorium* Germany 1920. Erich Kaiser-Titz (H) ?
66. *Das Haus ohne Fenster* Germany 1920.
67—81. Series made in GB in 1921, with Eille Norwood (H), Hubert Willis (W).
   The Dying Detective, The Devil's Foot, A Case of Identity, The Yellow Face, The Red-Headed League, The Resident Patient, A Scandal in Bohemia, The Man with the Twisted Lip, The Beryl Coronet, The Noble Bachelor, The Copper Beeches, The Empty House, The Tiger of San Pedro, The Priory School, The Solitary Cyclist.
82. *The Hound of the Baskervilles* GB 1921. Eille Norwood (H), Hubert Willis (W).
83—97. Series made in GB in 1922. Eille Norwood (H), Hubert Willis (W).
   Charles Augustus Milverton, The Abbey Grange, The Norwood Builder, The Reigate Squires, The Naval Treaty, The Second Stain, The Red Circle, The Six Napoleons, Black Peter, The Bruce-Partington Plans, The Stockbroker's Clerk, The Boscombe Valley Mystery, The Musgrave Ritual, The Golden Pince-Nez, The Greek Interpreter.
98. *Sherlock Holmes* USA 1922. John Barrymore (H), Roland Young (W).
99—113. Series made in GB in 1923. Eille Norwood (H), Hubert Willis (W).
   Silver Blaze, The Speckled Band, The Gloria Scott, The Blue Carbuncle, The Engineer's Thumb, His Last Bow, The Cardboard Box, Lady Frances Carfax, The Three Students, The Missing Three-Quarter, Thor Bridge, The Stone of Mazarin, The Dancing Men, The Crooked Man, The Final Problem.
114. *The Sign of Four* GB 1923. Eille Norwood (H), Arthur Cullin (W).
115. *Der Hund von Baskerville* Germany 1929. Carlyle Blackwell (H), Georges Seroff (W).

SOUND FILMS
116. *The Return of Sherlock Holmes* USA 1929. Clive Brook (H), H. Reeves Smith (W).

117. *Paramount on Parade* USA 1930. Clive Brook (H).
118. *The Sleeping Cardinal* GB 1931. Arthur Wontner (H), Ian Fleming (W).
119. *The Speckled Band* GB 1931. Raymond Massey (H), Athole Stewart (W).
120. *The Hound of the Baskervilles* GB 1932. Robert Rendel (H), Frederick Lloyd (W).
121. *The Missing Rembrandt* GB 1932. Arthur Wontner (H), Ian Fleming (W).
122. *The Sign of Four* GB 1932. Arthur Wontner (H), Ian Hunter (W).
123. *Sherlock Holmes* USA 1932. Clive Brook (H), Reginald Owen (W).
124. *Lelicek ve Sluzbach Sherlocka Holmese.* Czechoslovakia 1932. Martin Fric (H).
125. *A Study in Scarlet* USA 1933. Reginald Owen (H), Warburton Gamble (W).
126. *The Radio Murder Mystery* USA 1933. Richard Gordon (H).
127. *The Triumph of Sherlock Holmes* GB 1935. Arthur Wontner (H), Ian Fleming (W).
128. *Der Hund von Baskerville* Germany 1937. Bruno Güttner (H), Fritz Odemar (W).
129. *Sherlock Holmes: Die Graue Dame* Germany 1937. Hermann Speelmans (H).
130. *Silver Blaze* GB 1937. Arthur Wontner (H), Ian Fleming (W).
131. *Der Mann, der Sherlock Holmes war* Germany 1937. Hans Albers (H), Heinz Rühmann (W).
132. *The Hound of the Baskervilles* USA 1939. Basil Rathbone (H), Nigel Bruce (W).
133. *The Adventures of Sherlock Holmes* USA 1939. Basil Rathbone (H), Nigel Bruce (W).
134—145. Series made in USA, 1943 to 1946. Basil Rathbone (H), Nigel Bruce (W).
    Sherlock Holmes and the Voice of Terror, Sherlock Holmes and the Secret Weapon, Sherlock Holmes in Washington, Sherlock Holmes Faces Death, Spider Woman, The Scarlet Claw, The Pearl of Death, The House of Fear, The Woman in Green, Pursuit to Algiers, Terror by Night, Dressed to Kill.
146. *Sherlock Holmes Sieht dem Tod ins Gesicht* A German combination of *Spider Woman* and *Scarlet Claw*, above.
147. *Sherlock Holmes Jagt den Teufel von Soho* A German combination of *Sherlock Holmes Faces Death* and *The Pearl of Death*, above.
148. *The Speckled Band* USA 1949. TV Film. Alan Napier (H), Melville Cooper (W).
149. *The Man with the Twisted Lip* GB 1951. John Longden (H), Campbell Singer (W).
150—188. Series of 39 TV films made in France, 1954. Ronald Howard (H), Howard Marion Crawford (W).
    The Case of the Cunningham Heritage, Lady Beryl, The Winthrop Legend, The Mother Hubbard Case, The Pennsylvania Gun, The Red-Headed League, The Belligerent Ghost, The Thistle Killer, The Shoeless Engineer, The Shy Ballerina, The Deadly Prophecy, The Split Ticket, Harry Crocker, The Reluctant Carpenter, The Texas Cowgirl, The Laughing Mummy, The Diamond Tooth, Blind Man's Bluff, The Greystone Inscription, The French Interpreter, The Vanished Detective, The Careless Suffragette, The Baker Street Nursemaids, The Tyrant's Daughter, The Impostor Mystery, The Christmas Pudding, The Jolly Hangman, The Impromptu Performance, The Singing Violin, The Violent Suitor, The Night Train Riddle, The Perfect Husband, The Unlucky Gambler, The Exhumed

Client, *The Neurotic Detective, The Baker Street Bachelors, The Eiffel Tower, The Haunted Gainsborough, A Case of Royal Murder.*

189. *The Hound of the Baskervilles* GB 1959. Peter Cushing (H), Andre Morell (W).
190. *Sherlock Holmes und das Halsband des Todes* Germany 1962. Christopher Lee (H), Thorley Walters (W).
191. *A Study in Terror* GB 1965. John Neville (H), Donald Houston (W).
192. *L'ultimo dei Baskerville* Italy 1968. TV film. Nando Gazzolo (H).
193. *La valle della paura* Italy 1968. TV film. Nando Gazzolo (H).
194. *The Private Life of Sherlock Holmes* GB 1970. Robert Stephens (H), Colin Blakely (W).
195. *Touha Sherlocka Holmese* Czechoslovakia 1971. Radovan Lukavsky (H), Vaclav Voska (W).
196. *They might be Giants* USA 1972. George C. Scott (H), Joanne Woodward (W).
197. *The Hound of the Baskervilles* USA 1972. TV film. Stewart Granger (H), Bernard Fox (W).
198. *Monsieur Sherlok Holmes* France 1974. TV film.
199. *The Adventure of Sherlock Holmes' Smarter Brother* GB 1975. Douglas Wilmer (H), Thorley Walters (W).
200. *The Seven Per Cent Solution* GB 1976. Nicol Williamson (H), Robert Duval (W).

RADIO

1. *The Adventures of Sherlock Holmes* USA 1930–31. Series of 35 broadcasts. Richard Gordon (H), Leigh Lovell (W). First of series had William Gillette (H).
2. *The Adventures of Sherlock Holmes* USA 1931–2. 40 broadcasts. Richard Gordon (H), Leigh Lovell (W).
3. *The Adventures of Sherlock Holmes* USA 1932–33. 36 broadcasts. Richard Gordon (H), Leigh Lovell (W).
4. *The Adventures of Sherlock Holmes* USA 1934–35. 29 broadcasts. Louis Hector (H), Leigh Lovell (W).
5. *Sherlock Holmes* USA 1935. William Gillette (H), Reginald Mason (W).
6. *Sherlock Holmes* USA 1936. 48 broadcasts. Richard Gordon (H), Harry West (W).
7. *Sherlock Holmes* USA 1938. Orson Welles (H), Ray Collins (W).
8. *The Adventures of Sherlock Holmes* USA 1939–40. 24 broadcasts. Basil Rathbone (H), Nigel Bruce (W).
9. *Sherlock Holmes* USA 1940–46. 218 broadcasts. Basil Rathbone (H), Nigel Bruce (W).
10. *The Boscombe Valley Mystery* BBC 1943. Arthur Wontner (H), Carleton Hobbs (W).
11. *My Dear Watson* BBC 1943. John Cheatle (H), Ralph Truman (W).
12. *Sherlock Holmes and Dr. Watson* BBC 1944, and other schools broadcasts 1945, 1947, 1949 and 1950. Carleton Hobbs (H).
13. *The Speckled Band* BBC 1945. Sir Cedric Hardwicke (H), Finlay Currie (W).
14. *Silver Blaze* BBC 1945. Laidman Browne (H), Norman Shelley (W).
15. *The New Adventures of Sherlock Holmes* USA 1946–47. 39 broadcasts. Tom Conway (H), Nigel Bruce (W).
16. *Sherlock Holmes* USA 1947–48. 39 broadcasts. John Stanley (H), Alfred Shirley (W).
17. *Sherlock Holmes* USA 1948–49. 39 broadcasts. John Stanley (H),

Ian Martin (W).

18. *The Speckled Band* BBC 1948. Howard Marion Crawford (H), Finlay Currie (W).
19. *The Adventures of Sherlock Holmes* USA 1949–50. 39 broadcasts. Ben Wright (H), Eric Snowden (W).
20. *Sherlock Holmes Stories* BBC 1952–57. 17 broadcasts. Carleton Hobbs (H), Norman Shelley (W).
21. *Sherlock Holmes* BBC 1953. Carleton Hobbs (H), Norman Shelley (W).
22. *Tribute to Sherlock Holmes* BBC 1954. Alan Wheatley (H).
23. *The Adventures of Sherlock Holmes* BBC 1954. 12 broadcasts. John Gielgud (H), Ralph Richardson (W).
24. *The Hound of the Baskervilles* BBC 1958. Carleton Hobbs (H), Norman Shelley (W).
25. *Sherlock Holmes* BBC 1958. Hugh Manning (H), Leigh Crutchley (W).
26. *Sherlock Holmes* BBC 1959–69. 50 broadcasts. Carleton Hobbs (H), Norman Shelley (W).
27. *The Sign of Four* BBC 1959. Richard Hurndall (H), Bryan Coleman (W).
28. (*Sherlock Holmes*) Sweden 1959–60. 2 broadcasts. Georg Årlin (H), Ragnar Falck (W).
29. (*Sherlock Holmes Long Stories*) BBC 1960–63. 4 broadcasts. Carleton Hobbs (H), Norman Shelley (W).
30. (*Sherlock Holmes*) Switzerland 1967. 6 broadcasts. Marcel Imhoff (H).
31. *Masterdetectives* Sweden 1967. 2 broadcasts. Stig Ericsson (H).
32. *Baskervilles Hund* Sweden 1971. Georg Årlin (H), Gosta Pruzelius (W).
33. (*Sherlock Holmes*) Sweden 1974. 4 broadcasts. Jan Blomberg (H), Gosta Pruzelius (W).
34. *A Study in Scarlet* BBC 1974. Robert Powell (H), Dinsdale Landen (W).

TELEVISION

1. *The Three Garridebs* USA 1937. Louis Hector (H).
2. *Sherlock Holmes* USA 1950. Basil Rathbone (H).
3. *The Mazarin Stone* BBC 1951. Andrew Osborn (H), Philip King (W).
4. *Sherlock Holmes* BBC 1951. 6 programmes. Alan Wheatley (H), Raymond Francis (W).
5. *The Black Baronet* USA 1953. Basil Rathbone (H), Martyn Green (W).
6. *The Speckled Band* BBC 1964. Douglas Wilmer (H), Nigel Stock (W).
7. *Sherlock Holmes* BBC 1965. 12 programmes. Douglas Wilmer (H), Nigel Stock (W).
8. *Sherlock Holmes* BBC 1968. 16 programmes. Peter Cushing (H), Nigel Stock (W).
9. *Elementary My Dear Watson* BBC 1973. John Cleese (H), William Rushton (W).
10. *Dr. Watson and the Darkwater Hall Mystery* BBC 1974. Edward Fox (W).

Acknowledgements

My grateful thanks are due to many enthusiasts and collectors for help and friendship over a long period. Thanks also to those actors, directors and writers who were so generous with their time and patience: Colin Blakely, Clive Brook, Alfred Burke, Harry H. Corbett, Lord Donegall, Raymond Francis, Ronald Howard, Christopher Lee, Raymond Mander and Joe Mitchenson, the late Henry Oscar, Albert Parker, the late George Pearson, Peter Sallis, Norman Schatell, Robert Stephens, Alan Wheatley, Douglas Wilmer, the late Arthur Wontner and John Wood.

I must also thank Jacques Deslandes, Anthony Howlett, and Myrtil Frida of the Czech Film Institute for help with film stills and particularly Stanley Mackenzie and Richard Lancelyn Green for the loan of treasures from their remarkable collections.

The editor of *The Sherlock Holmes Journal* has kindly allowed me to adapt pieces originally written for that publication.

Finally I am obliged to Mary Pointer and Adelaide Griffin for all their kindnesses in preparation and typing.

Copyright of film stills and photographs belongs to the companies stated in the captions.

Index

Abbey Grange, The, 161
Adventure in the Life of Sherlock Holmes, An, 158
Adventure of Sherlock Holmes' Smarter Brother, The, 60, 163
Adventures of Sherlock Holmes, The, 50, 130, 160, 162–3
Aguja Hueca, La, 159
Alias Jimmy Valentine, 32
Alte Sekretär, Der, 160
Amis, Kingsley, 102–3
Arroyo, Enrique, 80
Arsène Lupin contra Sherlock Holmes, 35
Arsène Lupins Ende, 160
Aventures de Sherlock Holmes, Les, 160

Baker Street, 99, 127, 159
Baker Street Bachelors, The, 163
Baker Street Nursemaids, The, 163
Bank of England, The, 106, 158
Belligerent Ghost, The, 162
Beryl Coronet, The, 23, 160–1
Black Baronet, The, 164
Black Peter, 161
Blanched Soldier, The, 103
Blaue Diamant, Der, 160
Blind Man's Buff, 162
Blue Carbuncle, The, 18, 136, 161
Boscombe Valley Mystery, The, 9–10, 22, 160–1, 163
Brock, H. M., 13
Bruce-Partington Plans, The, 161
Burglar and the Lady, The, 159

Campbell, Dr Maurice, 143–4, 148
Captura de Raffles, La, 159
Cardboard Box, The, 120, 161
Careless Suffragette, The, 162
Case of Identity, A, 161
Case of Royal Murder, A, 163
Case of the Cunningham Heritage, The, 162
Case of the Metal Sheathed Elements, The, 129
Chaplin, Charles, 29, 31
Charles Augustus Milverton, 161
Christmas Pudding, The, 162
Copper Beeches, The, 160–1
Crooked Man, The, 161
Crown Diamond, The, 73, 107, 159
Cunard, Grace, 38–9

Dalton, Patsy, 139–40
Dalton, Philip, 137, 139, 145, 148
Dancing Men, The, 155, 161
Danvers-Walker, Bob, 138, 143
Deadly Prophecy, The, 162
Decourcelle, Pierre, 33–4
Devil's Foot, The, 161

Devil's Servant, The, 159
Diamond Tooth, The, 162
Dr Gar el Harma, 96
Dr Macdonald's Sanatorium, 161
Dr Watson and the Darkwater Hall Mystery, 102–3, 164
Donegall, the Marquis of, 139, 145
Dose des Kardinals, Die, 161
Doyle, Adrian Conan, 55, 140, 142–4, 153
Doyle, Sir Arthur Conan, 7–9, 11–12, 18, 28, 36, 39–40, 45–6, 65, 79–81, 95, 152–3
Drei Tage Tot, 161
Dressed to Kill, 162
Droske No. 519, 160
Dunkle Schloss, Das, 161
Dying Detective, The, 12, 14, 161

Eiffel Tower, The, 163
Einsame Haus, Das, 160
Elementary, My Dear Watson, 164
Elvey, Maurice, 81
Empty House, The, 106, 131, 161
Engineer's Thumb, The, 161
Erdstrommotor, Der, 161
Exhumed Client, The, 162

Falschen Rembrandts, Die, 160
Final Problem, The, 9, 11, 21, 106, 117, 147, 149, 152, 156, 161
Flucht, Die, 160
Ford, John, 38
Forlslaeate Barnepige, 160
French Interpreter, The, 162
Friston, D. H., 8–9

Garra de Holmes, La, 159
Giftplombe, Die, 160
Gloria Scott, The, 17, 161
Golden Pince-Nez, The, 161
Gore-Booth, Lady, 141, 148
Gore-Booth, Sir Paul, 135–6, 138, 148–9, 151–2
Graa Dame, Den, 160
Great Detective, The, 77, 158–9
Greek Interpreter, The, 161
Green, June Lancelyn, 137, 140, 148
Green, Roger Lancelyn, 137, 140, 148
Greene, Graham, 97
Greystone Inscription, The, 162
Griffard's Claw, 160

Hardwick, Michael, 139, 141–2, 145, 147–8, 152–3, 157
Hardwick, Mollie, 139, 142, 147, 157
Harry Crocker, 162
Haunted Gainsborough, The, 163
Haus Ohne Fenster, Das, 161
Hazanas de Sherlock Holmes, 159

Heart of London, The, 159
His Last Bow, 161
Holmes, Sherlock, actors as: Albers, Hans, 50, 162; Alstrup, Carl, 159; Anderson, Charters H., 159; Årlin, Georg, 164; Aylmer, Felix, 47, 159; Barrymore, John, 41–2, 96, 107, 161; Baur, Harry, 34, 159; Beecher, St John, 158; Benham, Harry, 71, 160; Bentley, Grendon, 159; Bergendorff, Hr, 66, 158; Bergvall, Hr, 66, 158; Birch, Vilhelm, 70, 158; Blackwell, Carlyle, 44–5, 82, 84, 161; Blake, John, 158; Blakiston, Clarence, 158; Bland, Sydney, 159; Bliss, Ernest, 158; Blomberg, Jan, 164; Bonn, Ferdinand, 33, 80, 159–61; Bradford, Herbert, 67, 159; Brady, Brandon, 160; Bragington, James, 37–8, 117, 160; Brenckendorff, Kurt, 161; Brook, Clive, 45–6, 96–7, 107, 110–11, 118, 161–2; Brookfield, Charles, 26–7, 158; Browne, Laidman, 163; Buckmaster, Charles, 159; Burg, Eugen, 161; Burke, Alfred, 54–5, 158; Butler, Richard, 158; Carter, Lawrence, 158; Chambers, Hubert S., 158; Cheatle, John, 163; Cleese, John, 164; Cliffe, H. Cooper, 159; Comes, Sr, 159; Conway, Charles, 68, 158; Conway, Tom, 163; Corbett, Harry H., 60–1, 159; Costello, Maurice, 160; Crawley, J. S., 158; Cushing, Peter, 59–60, 89, 92, 100, 133, 163–4; Dacre, Henry S., 158; Deane, Hamilton, 158; Dorph-Petersen, 68, 115, 158; Edwards, Geoffrey, 75, 159; Edwards, Walter, 158; Ericsson, Stig, 164; Felton, William, 158; Flink, Hugo, 72, 161; Florents, Herman, 158–9; Ford, Francis, 38–9, 160; Foster, Bryan, 160; Franklin, Richard, 64–5, 160; Fric, Martin, 74, 162; Froberg, Einar, 159; Gazzolo, Nando, 163; Gee, Donald, 65, 159; Gémier, Firmin, 33–4, 159; Gielgud, John, 156, 164; Gilbert, Robert, 159; Gillette, William, 15, 26–31, 33, 41, 158, 161, 163; Glover, Julian, 65, 78, 159; Goodyer-Kettley, R., 159; Gordon, Richard, 162–3; Gouget, Henri, 160; Grain, A. Corney, 159; Granger, Stewart, 93–4, 129, 163; Guixer, Sr, 159; Güttner, Bruno, 48, 87–8, 97, 162; Hardwicke, Cedric, 163; Hardy, Robert, 157; Hastings, Cuyler, 158; Hatch, Roger, 160; Heathcott, Roger, 128, 159; Hector, Louis, 163–4; Heggie, O. P., 159; Henry, George, 158; Hobbs, Carleton, 163–4;

Holmes, Sherlock, actors as—*contd.*
Holland, Harold, 158; Horgan, Patrick, 158; Howard, Ronald, 55, 57, 113, 125, 133, 162; Howlett, Noel, 158; Hurndall, Richard, 164; Imhoff, Marcel, 159; Johnson, Arthur V., 159; Karoly, Bauman, 160; Kelcey, Herbert, 158; Kennedy, Edmund, 159; Lagoni, Otto, 69, 158; Larsson, William, 158; Lawson, John, 158; Lee, Christopher, 56–8, 89–90, 113, 126, 163; Lester, Charles H., 158; Leyton, H. Lawrence, 30–1, 158; Lister, Rupert, 159; Ljungqvist, Emil, 158; Longden, John, 162; Lukarvsky, Radovan, 76, 163; Lynn, Carl, 159; Macmillan, Kenneth, 77, 159; Manning, Hugh, 164; Massey, Raymond, 73, 162; Millward, Charles, 159; Moore, Alan, 77, 159; Moore, Eugene, 158; Myin, Marcel, 66, 158; Napier, Alan, 162; Neilson, Harold V., 159; Neilson-Terry, Dennis, 73, 159; Neuss, Alwin, 35–6, 81, 160–1; Neville, John, 61–2, 114, 127, 158, 163; Norwood, Eille, 39–41, 81–2, 107–9, 117–18, 159, 161; Nyblom, Knut, 66, 116, 158; Olivar, Sr, 159; Osborn, Andrew, 164; Oscar, Henry, 42–4, 159; Owen, Reginald, 46, 162; Parreno, Sr, 159; Perceval, W. R., 158; Pollitt, Clyde, 160; Powell, Robert, 164; Preece, Tim, 78, 92, 159; Preston, John F., 158; Prevost, Nicholas le, 160; Rasmussen, Holgar, 160; Rathbone, Basil, 50–2, 87–8, 94, 98–9, 107–8, 112, 132, 159, 162–4; Redgrave, Roy, 158; Rendel, Robert, 85, 162; Renouf, Henry, 158; Rivington, Kenneth, 28, 158; Ronnblad, Hugo, 158; Royce, Julian, 28–30, 158–9; Saintsbury, H. A., 28–31, 33, 158–9, 161; Sargent, Fred, 158; Schmidt, Albrecht, 158; Schwarwenlsa, Franz, 158; Scott, Cyril, 159; Scott, George C., 60–1, 163; Seymour, Walter R., 158; Shannon, T. A., 158; Slaughter, Tod, 159; Speelmans, Herman, 49, 162; Stanley, John, 163; Stanton, Herbert, 159; Stephens, Robert, 62–5, 128, 134, 158, 163; Stewart, H. Hamilton, 31–3, 158; Stirling, Edward, 42, 44, 159; Tremayne, Leonard, 158; Treville, Georges, 36–7, 107, 160; Trood, Leo, 158; Vaughan, E. Vassal Vaughan, 159; Verkade, Eduard, 158; Vries, Henry de, 41, 159; Warwick, Robert, 158; Weaver, Fritz, 127, 157, 159; Webb, John, 158; Welles, Orson, 75, 156, 163; Wheatley, Alan, 18, 52, 54, 58, 100, 124, 164; Williams, Bransby, 158; Williamson, Nicol, 163; Wilmer, Douglas, 58–60, 100, 102, 163–4; Wontner, Arthur, 18, 46, 49, 107, 162–3; Wood, John, 18, 62–3, 65, 107, 162–3; Wright, Ben, 164; Wulff, Emil, 159; Wylie, John, 160; York, C., 159; York, Charles, 159; Young, H. A., 159
Holmes y Rafles, 159
Holmeses of Baker Street, The, 47, 159
Holroyd, James, 136–7, 139
Hotel Mysterierul, 160
Hound of the Baskervilles, The, 11–12, 23, 25, 50, 78–94, 99, 105, 112, 129, 159–64

House of Fear, The, 162
Houseboat on the Styx, The, 159
Howlett, Anthony, 138, 142–4, 148–9, 152–3
Hund von Baskerville, Der, play, 33, 80, 159; films, 36, 45, 48–9, 59, 81–2, 85–7, 160–2
Hvem er Hun, 160

Imposter Mystery, The, 162
Impromptu Performance, The, 162
Indische Spinne, Die, 161

Jolly Hangman, The, 162
Jover, Gonzalo, 80

Kaiser-Titz, Erich, 161
Kasette, Die, 161
Kunz, Albert, 136, 139–42, 146–9

Lady Beryl, 162
Lady Frances Carfax, 137, 161
Latest Triumph of Sherlock Holmes, The, 160
Laughing Mummy, The, 162
Lejeune, C. A., 53
Lelicek ve Sluzbach Sherlocka Holmese, 74, 162

Mann, der Sherlock Holmes war, Der, 97, 162
Man With the Twisted Lip, The, 24, 161–2
Mazarin Stone, The, 107, 161, 164
Medlem af den Sorte Hand, 160
Memories and Adventures, 40
Millionobligation, 160
Missing Rembrandt, The, 162
Missing Three-Quarter, The, 161
Monsieur Sherlock Holmes, 163
Mord im Splendid Hotel, Der, 161
Mother Hubbard Case, The, 162
Musgrave Ritual, The, 160–1
My Dear Watson, 163

Nadie Mas Fuerte Que Sherlock Holmes, 159
Naval Treaty, The, 12, 19–20, 161
Neill, Roy William, 51
Neurotic Detective, The, 163
Night Train Riddle, The, 162
Night With the Stars, A, 159
Noble Bachelor, The, 7, 161
Norwood Builder, The, 161

Oswald, Richard, 81–6

Paget, Sidney, 8–14, 17–25
Paget, Walter, 8–9, 12, 14
Painful Predicament of Sherlock Holmes, The, 158
Paramount on Parade, 162
Parker, Albert, 41–2
Pearl of Death, The, 162
Pearson, George, 37–8
Pennsylvania Gun, The, 162
Perfect Husband, The, 162
Pointer, Mary, 139, 142, 155
Pointer, Michael, 139, 148
Priory School, The, 161
Private Life of Sherlock Holmes, The, 62, 65, 99–100, 123, 128, 134, 163
Pursuit to Algiers, 162

Radio Murder Mystery, The, 162
Raedsom Nat, En, 160

Raffle-ing of Sherlock Holmes, The, 159
Red Circle, The, 161
Red-Headed League, The, 13, 20, 160–1
Reigate Squires, The, 20, 160–1
Reluctant Carpenter, The, 162
Resident Patient, The, 161
Return of Sherlock Holmes, The, 12, 39, 40–1, 45–6, 75, 109–10, 118, 159, 161
Reynolds, Sheldon, 55, 57
Rival Sherlock Holmes, 160
Robinson, Fletcher, 80
Rotterdam-Amsterdam, 35, 161

Sangerindens Diamanter, 160
Scandal in Bohemia, A, 10, 106, 108, 161
Scarlet Claw, The, 162
Schicksal der Renate Yongk, Das, 161
Schlangenring, Der, 161
Schlau, Schlauer, am Schlauesten, 160
Scholefield, Charles, 145, 151, 153
Schrei in der Nacht, 36, 161
Second Stain, The, 161
Seyffertitz, Gustav von, 42
Sheerluck Jones, 158
Sherlock Holmes, films (1908), 117, 160; (1909–10), 160; (1916), 28, 161; (1922), 41–2, 161; (1932), 45–6, 111, 118, 162; Bell sketch, 158; Bonn play, 33, 159; Decourcelle play, 33–4, 159; Felton sketch, 158; Gillette play, 26–32, 41, 62–3, 65–6, 68–70, 96, 104, 106–7, 116, 123, 130, 158, 160–1; Oakley play, 160; Ottomeyer play, 159; Rahnheld play, 159; Rathbone play, 52, 159; Rogers play, 96, 106, 158; Schontau play, 158; Weiss play, 159
Sherlock Holmes and Dr Watson, 163
Sherlock Holmes and the Affair of the Amorous Regent, 159
Sherlock Holmes and the Secret Weapon, 162
Sherlock Holmes and the Speckled Band, 128, 159
Sherlock Holmes and the Voice of Terror, 162
Sherlock Holmes auf Urlaub, 161
Sherlock Holmes Baffled, 70, 160
Sherlock Holmes contra Dr Mors, 33, 160
Sherlock Holmes contra Professor Moryarty, 34–5, 160
Sherlock Holmes, Detective, 158
Sherlock Holmes: Die Graue Dame, 49–50, 162
Sherlock Holmes Faces Death, 162
Sherlock Holmes I Bonderfangerklør, 160
Sherlock Holmes I Livsfare, 160
Sherlock Holmes in Gebirge, 159
Sherlock Holmes in Scandal in Bohemia, 160
Sherlock Holmes in Washington, 162
Sherlock Holmes jagt den Teufel von Soho, 162
Sherlock Holmes nächtliche Begegnung, 161
Sherlock Holmes of Baker Street, 64–5, 160
Sherlock Holmes Returns, 160
Sherlock Holmes sicht dem Tod ins Gesicht, 162
Sherlock Holmes Solves the Sign of the Four, 71, 160
Sherlock Holmes und das Halsband des Todes, 58, 113, 126, 163
Sherlock's Last Case, 65, 78, 102, 159

Shoeless Engineer, The, 162
Shoscombe Old Place, 13, 16
Shy Ballerina, The, 162
Sign of (the) Four, The, 8, 79, 97, 100, 107, 122, 158, 161–2, 164
Silver Blaze, 11, 160–3
Singing Violin, The, 162
Six Napoleons, The, 161
Sleeping Cardinal, The, 46–7, 162
Solitary Cyclist, The, 161
Speckled Band, The, 22, 29–31, 42–4, 58, 65–6, 73, 77, 96, 106–7, 122–3, 159–64
Spider Woman, 112, 162
Split Ticket, The, 162
Steele, Frederic Dorr, 13, 15–16, 18
Stockbrokers Clerk, The, 161
Stolen Papers, The, 160
Strand Magazine, The, 8–9, 11–14, 40, 79
Stuart Keen, 96
Study in Scarlet, A, 8–9, 24, 37–9, 46, 79, 117, 159–60, 164
Study in Terror, A, 61–2, 102, 114, 127, 163
Surelock Holmes, 158

Terror by Night, 162
Texas Cowgirl, The, 162
They Might be Giants, 60–1, 159, 163
Thistle Killer, The, 162
Thor Bridge, 161
Three Garridebs, The, 164
Three Students, The, 161
Tiger of San Pedro, The, 161
Touha Sherlocka Holmese, 76, 163
Tragedia de Baskerville, La, 80, 159
Tribute to Sherlock Holmes, 164
Triumph of Sherlock Holmes, The, 47, 162
Twidle, Arthur, 13
Tyrant's Daughter, The, 162

Ultimo dei Baskerville, l', 163
Under the Clock, 26, 158
Unheimliche Zimmer, Das, 160
Unlucky Gambler, The, 162

Valle della paura, La, 163
Valley of Fear, The, 12, 14, 29, 47, 79, 161
Vanished Detective, The, 162
Nededor de Cadaveres, El, 159
Violent Suitor, The, 162

Was er im Spiegel sah, 161
Watson, Dr, actors as: Bayliss, Peter, 78, 102, 159; Blakely, Colin, 63–4, 99–100, 128, 134, 163; Bruce, Nigel, 50–2, 87–8, 94, 98–100, 102, 132, 162–3; Bunnage, Avis, 159; Coleman, Bryan, 164; Collins, Ray, 163; Cooper, Melville, 162; Crawford, Howard Marion, 55, 57, 104, 113, 125, 133, 162, 164; Crutchley, Leigh, 164; Cullin, Arthur, 161; Currie, Finlay, 163–4; Daneman, Paul, 104; Dawson, Ivo, 159; Duvall, Robert, 163; Dwyer, Frank, 160; Falck, Ragnar, 164; Fielding, Edward, 161; Fleming, Ian, 46, 97, 162; Fox, Bernard, 93, 129, 163; Fox, Edward, 102, 164; Francis, Raymond, 53, 100, 164; Gamble, Warburton, 162; Green, Martyn, 164; Hamund, St John, 158; Hare, F. Lumsden, 158; Hart, J., 159; Hicks, Seymour, 26, 158; Holden, Stanley, 159; Houston, Donald, 61, 101–2, 127, 163; Hunter, Ian, 97, 162; Keating, Michael, 77; King, Claude, 159; King, Philip, 164; Landen, Dinsdale, 164; Lloyd, Frederick, 85, 162; Lovell, Leigh, 163; Lyndal, Percy, 29, 158; McKay, John, 159; McRae, Bruce, 158; Martin, Ian, 164; Mason, Reginald, 163; Matthews, Martin, 160; Morell, Andre, 59, 89, 105, 163; Mouleton, Patrick, 160; Odemar, Fritz, 89, 97, 162; Owen, Reginald, 97, 162; Pitts, William, 160; Playfair, Nigel, 159; Pruzelius, Gosta, 164; Raine, Jack, 159; Rawley, Joseph, 158; Rhoades, Terry, 160; Richardson, Ralph, 156, 164; Rühmann, Heinz, 50, 97, 162; Rushton, William, 164; Russell, E. Wensley, 159; Rust, Clive, 128, 159; Saillard, 159; Sallis, Peter, 99–100, 127, 159; Salom, Sr, 159; Seerle, Carl Smith, 158; Seroff, Georges, 84, 161; Shelley, Norman, 163–4; Shirley, Alfred, 163; Singer, Campbell, 162; Simpson, Richard, 92, 159; Socias, Sr, 159; Smith, H. Reeves, 45, 96–7, 161; Snowden, Eric, 164; Stewart, Athole, 73, 162; Stock, Nigel, 58, 100, 101, 157, 164; Stoker, H. G., 118, 159; Stringer, Nick, 160; Taylour, R. V., 159; Thomson, Lionel, 160; Truman, Ralph, 163; Voska, Vaclav, 76, 163; Walters, Thorley, 56–7, 126, 163; West, Harry, 163; Willis, Hubert, 82, 96, 117, 161; Wingfield, Conway, 159; Woodward, Joanne, 60, 163; Wykeham, Reginald, 158; Young, Roland, 96, 161
William Voss, 161
Winthrop Legend, The, 162
Weight, Michael, 120, 122
Wells, H. G., 79
Wie Enstand der Hund von Baskerville, 160
Wilder, Gener, 60
Wiles, Frank, 12–14, 16
Woman in Green, The, 162

Yellow Face, The, 17, 161